Conversation guide
Spanish

Published by:
Editorial Stanley

Illustrated by:
Daniel Redondo

First page design:
Diseño Irunés

© *Editorial Stanley*
Apdo. 207 - 20302 IRUN - ESPAÑA
Telf. (943) 64 04 12 - Fax. (943) 64 38 63

ISBN: 84-7873-299-3
Dep. Leg. BI-2634-03

First edition 1996
Reprinted 1997
Reprinted 1998
Reprinted 2003

Printers:
Imprenta Berekintza

Pronunciation

In order to achieve an approximation to the phonetics of some Spanish words it is necessary to resort to complicated phonetic symbols; for that reason, the use of a pocket book such as our Conversation Guide, would be very restricted. The user would have first to memorize all the phonetic symbols before being able to use the book.

Our aim is not, therefore, to teach the travel(l)er correct pronounciation, but, to attain that, using the normal English letters, s/he may make himself/herself understood in any Spanish-speaking country.

In some cases we have preferred to sacrifice the possibility of a smart Castilian pronounciation for another, less smart perhaps, but more within reach of an English-speaking person.

Contents

At the customs **En la aduana**		
Have you anything to declare?	**¿Tiene algo que declarar?**	Tyaynay ahlgoa kay dayklharahr?
I have nothing to declare.	**No tengo nada que declarar.**	Noa tayngoa nahdah kay dayklharahr.
I only have some presents.	**Sólo tengo unos regalos.**	Soaloa tayngoa oonoahss raygahloas.
Which is your luggage?	**¿Cuál es su equipaje?**	Kwahl ayss soo aykeepahkhay?
How many cases do you have?	**¿Cuántas maletas tienen ustedes?**	Kwahntass mahlaytahs tyaynayn oostaydhess?
We have three cases.	**Tenemos tres maletas.**	Taynaymoass trayss mahlaytahs.
How many cigarettes?	**¿Cuántos cigarrillos?**	Kwahntoass theegahrreelyoass?
I have two hundred cigarettes.	**Tengo doscientos cigarrillos.**	Tayngoa dosthyayntoass theegahrreelyoas.
How many bottles of liquor?	**¿Cuántas botellas de licor?**	Kwahntass boataylyahss day leekor?
I have a bottle of brandy and a bottle of whisky.	**Tengo una botella de coñac y una de whisky.**	Tayngoa oonah boataylyah day konyak ee oonah day weeskee.
Are you on holiday?	**¿Está usted de vacaciones?**	Aystah oostdayd day bahkahthyonayss?
I'm on business.	**Estoy en viaje de negocios.**	Aystoy ayn byahkhay day naygoathyoass.
You will have to pay duty on this.	**Tendrá que pagar aduana por esto.**	Teyndrah kay pahgahr ahdwahnah porr aystoa.
Open this case, please.	**Abra esta maleta, por favor.**	Ahbrah aystah mahlaytah, porr fahbor.
Where's Information?	**¿Dónde está Informaciones?**	Doanday aystah eenformahthyoness?

My baggage has not arrived.	**Mi equipaje no ha llegado.**	Mee aykeepahkhay noa ah lyaygahdhoa?
One case is missing.	**Falta una maleta.**	Fahltah oonah mahlaytah.
Where are the luggage lockers?	**¿Dónde está consigna?**	Doanday aystah konseegnah?
Take these cases to a taxi.	**Lleve estas maletas a un taxi.**	Lyaybay aystahss mahlaytahs ah oon tahksee.
Where are the baggage trolleys?	**¿Dónde están los carritos del equipaje?**	Doanday aystahn loss kahrreetoss dayl aykeepahkhay?
Where's the information bureau?	**¿Dónde está informaciones?**	Doanday aystah eenformahthyoness?

Your passport, please.	**Su pasaporte, por favor.**	Soo pahssahportay, porr fahbhor.
May I see your papers?	**¿Me enseña su documentación?**	May aynsaynyah soo dokoomentahthyon?
Here's my passport.	**Aquí tiene mi pasaporte.**	Ahkee tyaynay mee pahssahportay.
My wife travels with me.	**Mi esposa viaja conmigo.**	Mee ayspoasah byahkah konmeegoa.
¿How long are you staying?	**¿Cuánto tiempo se va a quedar?**	Kwantoa tyaynpoa say bah ah keydahr?
I'll be staying...	**Me quedaré...**	May keydahreh....
a few days.	**unos días.**	oonoass deeahss.
two weeks.	**dos semanas.**	doss saymahnahss.
I'm travel(l)ing alone.	**Viajo solo.**	Byahkoh soaloa.
I'm American.	**Soy norteamericano.**	Soy nortayahmayreekahnoa.
Where are you staying?	**¿Dónde se hospeda?**	Doanday say ospehdhah?
What's your address in...?	**¿Cuál es su dirección en...?**	Kwahl ayss soo deeraykthyon ayn...?
Are you together?	**¿Están ustedes juntos?**	Aystahn oostaydhayss hoontoss?

I'm just passing through.	**Estoy de paso.**	Aystoy day pahssoh.

Vocabulary - Vocabulario

customs	**aduanas**	ahdwahnahs
anything	**algo**	ahlgoa
bag	**bolsa**	bolsah
bottle	**botella**	boataylyah
trolley	**carrito**	kahreetoa
cigarettes	**cigarrillos**	theegahrreelyoass
brandy	**coñac**	koanyak
to declare	**declarar**	dayklahrahr
duty	**derechos de aduana**	dayraychoass day ahdwahnah
papers	**documentación**	dokoomentathyon
luggage	**equipaje**	aykeepahkhay
missing	**falta**	fahltah
spirits	**licores**	leekorayss
suitcase	**maleta**	mahlaytah
camera	**máquina fotográfica**	mahkeenah foatoagrahfeekah
porter	**mozo**	moathoa
nothing	**nada**	nahdhah
business	**negocios**	naygothyoass
to pay	**pagar**	pahgahr
passport	**pasaporte**	pahssahportay
gift	**regalo**	raygahloa
tobacco	**tabaco**	tahbahkoh
holidays	**vacaciones**	bahkahthyonayss
to travel	**viajar**	byahkar
traveller	**viajero**	byahkhayroa

Hotels & boarding houses
Hoteles y pensiones

Where is there a good hotel?	¿Dónde hay un buen hotel?	Doanday igh oon bwayn oatehl?
Is there a boarding house in this place?	¿Hay alguna pensión en este sitio?	Igh ahlgoonah paynsyon ayn aystay sitioa?
Do you have a room?	¿Tienen ustedes una habitación?	Tyaynayn oostaydhays oonah ahbheetahthyon?
I want a single room with a shower.	Quiero una habitación individual con ducha.	Kyayroa oonah ahbheetahthyon indibidooahl kon doochah.
I want a double room with a bath.	Quiero una habitación doble con baño.	Kyayroa oonah ahbheetahthyon doablay kon bahnyoa.
We want a room for three days.	Queremos una habitación para tres días.	Kayraymoass oohan ahbheetahthyon pahrah trays deeahss.
We've reserved a room.	Hemos reservado una habitación.	Ehmoass rayssayrbahdhoa oonah ahbheetahthyon.
I want a quiet room.	Quiero una habitación tranquila.	Kyayroa oonah ahbheetahthyon trahnkeelah.
May I see the room?	¿Puedo ver la habitación?	Pwaydhoa behr lah ahbheetahthyon?
Do you have a room on the first floor?	¿Tiene usted alguna habitación en el primer piso?	Tyaynnay oostaydh ahlgoonah ahbheetahthyon ayn ayl preemayr peessoa?
A room looking on to the sea.	Una habitación que dé al mar.	Oonah ahbheetahthyon kay day ahl mahr.

Hotels & boarding houses - Hoteles y pensiones

We want a twin bedded room.	**Queremos una habitación con dos camas.**	Kayraymoass oonah ahbheetahthyon kon doss kahmahss
How much is the room per day?	**¿Cuánto es la habitación por día?**	Kwantoa ayss la ahbheetahthyon porr deeah?
Do you have something cheaper?	**¿Tiene algo más barato?**	Tyaynay ahlgoa mahss bahrahtoa?
Are meals included?	**¿Están incluidas las comidas?**	Aystahn eenklooedhass lahss koameedhahss?
How much is full board?	**¿Cuánto es la pensión completa?**	Kwantoa ayss lah paynsyon konplaytah?
Is there a television/phone in the room?	**¿Hay televisión / teléfono en la habitación?**	Igh taylaybheessyon/ taylayfoanoa ayn lah ahbheetahthyon?
I want a room with a balcony.	**Quiero una habitación con balcón.**	Kyayroa oohan ahbheetahthyon kon bahlkon.
Can we have bed and breakfast?	**¿Podemos tener habitación con desayuno?**	Poadhaymoass tenerr ahbhetahthyon kon daysahyoonoa?
Do you have a room with a better view?	**¿Tiene alguna habitación con mejor vista?**	Tyaynay ahlgoonah ahbheetahthyon kon mehkor beestah?
Fill in the registration form.	**Rellene el impreso.**	Raylyenay ayl impresso.
It's too expensive.	**Es demasiado caro.**	Ayss daymahssyahdhoa kahroa.
Do you want my passport?	**¿Quiere mi pasaporte?**	Kyaray mee pahssahportay?

Vocabulary - Vocabulario

per day	**al día**	ahl deeah
balcony	**balcón**	bahlkon
expensive	**caro**	kahroa
meal	**comida**	koameedhah
too	**demasiado**	daymahssyahdhoa
breakfast	**desayuno**	dayssahyoonoa
double	**doble**	doablay

twin	**gemela**	haymaylah
room	**habitación**	ahbheetahthyon
registration form	**impreso**	eemprayssoa
included	**incluido**	eenklooeedhoa
single	**individual**	eendeebeedooahl
cheaper	**más barata**	mahss bahrahtah
boarding house	**pensión**	paynsyon
full board	**pensión completa**	paynsyon komplaytah
looking on	**que dé**	kay day
reserve	**reservar**	rayssayrbahrr
quiet	**tranquila**	trankeelah
see	**ve**	bay

General requirements - Peticiones generales

What's our room number?	**¿Cuál es el número de nuestra habitación?**	Kwahl ayss ayl noomayroa day nwaystrah ahbheetahthyon?
Do you have a car park?	**¿Tienen ustedes aparcamiento?**	Tyaynayn oostaydhays ahparkamyentoa?
Can I have my key, please?	**¿Me da mi llave, por favor?**	May dah mee lyahbhay, porr fahbhor?
Does the hotel have a garage?	**¿Tiene garaje el hotel?**	Tyaynay gahrahkhay ayl oatehl?
Can we have the meals in the room?	**¿Podemos tomar las comidas en la habitación?**	Poadhaymoass toamahr lahss koameedhahss ayn lah ahbheetahthyon?
What time is breakfast?	**¿A qué hora es el desayuno?**	Ah kay oorah ayss ayl dayssahyoonoa?
Where's the beauty salon?	**¿Dónde está el salón de belleza?**	Doanday aystah ayl sahlon day baylyaythah?
Is there a hairdresser's at the hotel?	**¿Hay peluquería en el hotel?**	Igh paylookayreeah ayn ayl oatehl?
Where's the lift?	**¿Dónde está el ascensor?**	Doanday aystah ayl ahsthaynsoar?

Is there a toilet on this floor?	¿Hay servicios en esta planta?	Ihg sayrbeethyoass ayn aystah plahntah?
Can I leave this in your safe?	¿Puedo dejar esto en su caja fuerte?	Pwaydhoa daykhar aystoa ayn soo kahkhah fwehrtay?
We need an extra pillow/blanket.	Necesitamos otra almohada/manta.	Naythayseetahmoass oatrah ahlmo-aahdhah/mahntah
We don't have a bath towel.	No tenemos toalla de baño.	Noa taynaymoass toaahlyah day bahnyoa.
Where's the dining-room?	¿Dónde está el comedor?	Doanday aystah ayl koamaydhor?
Is there a telephone on the ground floor?	¿Hay teléfono en la planta baja?	Igh taylayfoanoa ayn lah plahntah bahka?
Can we have a baby-sitter?	¿Nos pueden mandar un canguro?	Noass pwaydhayn mahndahrr oon kahngooroa?
Please, wake me up at...	Por favor, despiérteme a las...	Por fahbhor, dayspyayrtehmay ah lahs..
I want to see the manager.	Quiero ver al gerente.	Kyayroa bayr ahl khayrayntay.
When will the maid come?	¿Cuándo vendrá la señora de la limpieza?	Kwahndoa bayndrah lah saynyoorah day lah leempyaytha?
I need a typewriter and a tape recorder.	Necesito una máquina de escribir y una grabadora.	Naythayseetoa oonah mahkeenah day ayskreebheer ee oonah ghrabadoarah.

Vocabulary - Vocabulario

pillow	almohada	ahlmoaahdhah
car park	aparcamiento	aparkahmyentoa
lift	ascensor	ahsthaynsoar
safe	caja fuerte	kahkhah fwehrtay
baby-sitter	canguro	kangooroa
dining-room	comedor	koamaydhor
meals	comidas	koameedhahss

wake me up	**despiérteme**	dayspyayrtehmay
manager	**director**	deerehktoar
blanket	**manta**	mahntah
typewriter	**máquina de escribir**	mahkeenah day ayskreebheer
hairdresser's	**peluquería**	paylookayreeah
floor	**piso**	peessoa
beauty salon	**salón de belleza**	sahlon day baylaythah
maid	**señora de la limpieza**	saynyoarah day lah leempyaytha
toilet	**servicios**	sayrbeethyoass
bath towel	**toalla de baño**	toaahlyah day bahnyoa
tape recorder	**grabadora**	ghrabadoarah

Room service - Servicio de habitaciones

The television is not working.	**La televisión no funciona**	Lah taylaybheessyon noa foonthyoanah.
There's no soap.	**No hay jabón.**	Noa igh khahbhon.
There's no hot water.	**No hay agua caliente.**	Noa igh ahgwah kahlyayntay.
There's no toilet paper.	**No hay papel higiénico.**	Noa igh pahpehl eekhyayneekoa.
There are no towels.	**No hay toallas.**	Noa igh toaahlyahss.
The lavatory doesn't flush.	**La cadena del cuarto de baño no funciona.**	Lah kahdhaynah dayl kwahrtoa day bahnyoa noa foonthyoanah.
There are no ash-trays in the room.	**No hay ceniceros en la habitación.**	Noa igh thayneethayroass ayn lah ahbheetahthyon.
The lamp doesn't work.	**La lámpara no funciona.**	Lah lahmpahrah noa foonthyoanah.
Do you have laundry service?	**¿Hay servicio de lavandería?**	Igh sehrbeethyoa day lahbhahndayreeah?
Can we have break-fast in the room?	**¿Podemos desa-yunar en la habita-ción?**	Poadhaymoass dayssahyoonahr ayn lah ahbheetahthyon?
Can the heating be turned up/down?	**¿Se puede subir/bajar la calefac-ción?**	Say pwayday soobyrr/bahkhar lah kahlayfahkthyon?

The air conditioning doesn't work.	**El aire acondicionado no funciona.**	Ayl ighray ahkondeethyoanahdhoa noa foonthyoanah.
May I have another blanket?	**¿Me da otra manta?**	May dah oatrah mahntah?
How long will the laundry take?	**¿Cuánto tiempo tarda la lavandería?**	Kwahntoa tyaympoa tahrdah lah lahbhahndayreeah?
Can I have this suit pressed?	**¿Me pueden planchar este traje?**	May pwaydhayn plahnchahr aystay trahkay?
Do you have a needle and thread?	**¿Tienen aguja e hilo?**	Tyaynayn ahgookha ay eeloa?
Give me a call at eight o'clock.	**Llámeme a las ocho.**	Lyahmaymay ah lahs oachoa.
My key, please.	**La llave, por favor.**	Lah lyahbhay, porr fahbhor.
Are there any letters for me?	**¿Hay cartas para mí?**	Igh kahrtahs pahrah mee?
Are there any messages for me?	**¿Hay algún mensaje para mí?**	Igh ahlgoon maynssahkay pahrah mee?
Do you have writing paper/stamps / envelopes?	**¿Tienen papel de escribir/sellos/ sobres?**	Tyaynayn pahpehl day ayskreebher/ saylyoass/soabrayss?
What time is breakfast/lunch/dinner?	**¿A qué hora es el desayuno/la comida/la cena?**	Ah kay oarah ayss ayl dayssahyoanoa/ koameedhah/lah thaynah?

Vocabulary - Vocabulario

needle	**aguja**	ahgookha
safe	**caja fuerte**	kahkhah fwehrtay
heating	**calefacción**	kahlayfahkthyon
ashtray	**cenicero**	thayneethayroa
how long	**cuánto tiempo**	kwahntoa tyaympoa
breakfast	**desayuno**	dayssahyoonoa
to work	**funcionar**	foonthyoanahr

thread	**hilo**	eeloa
soap	**jabón**	khahbhon
laundry	**lavandería**	lahbhahndayreeah
call	**llamada**	lyahmahday
key	**llave**	lyahbhay
blanket	**manta**	mahntah
messages	**mensajes**	maynssahkayss
writing paper	**papel de escribir**	pahpehl day ayskreebheer
toilet paper	**papel higiénico**	pahpehl eekhyayneekoa
to press	**planchar**	plahnchahr
lavatory	**retrete**	raytraytay
to leave	**salir**	sahlyrr
stamps	**sellos**	saylyoass
envelopes	**sobres**	soabrayss
turn up/ down	**subir/bajar**	soobyrr/bahkahr
to take	**tardar, llevar**	tahrdahr, lyebahr
towels	**toallas**	toaahlyahss

Paying the bill - Pagando la cuenta

We are leaving to-morrow morning.	**Nos vamos mañana por la mañana**	Noas bahmoass mahnyahnah porr lah mahnyahnah.
Can I have my bill ready?	**¿Me prepara la cuenta?**	May praypahrah lah kwayntah?
What time must we check out?	**¿A qué hora debemos desocupar la habitación?**	Ah kay oarah day-baymoass dayssoa-koopahr lah ahbheetahthyon?
Is tax included?	**¿Están incluidos los impuestos?**	Aystahn eenkloo-eedhoass loass eempwaystoass?
Can you call a taxi?	**¿Puede llamar a un taxi?**	Pwayday lyahmahr ah oon taksee?
Do you accept credit cards?	**¿Acepta tarjetas de crédito?**	Ahthayptah tahrkaytahss day kraydheetoa?

Can I leave the luggage here until this afternoon?	**¿Puedo dejar el equipaje aquí hasta esta tarde?**	Pwaydoa daykhar ayl aykeepahkhay ahkee ahstah aystah tahrday?
We have had a pleasant stay.	**Hemos tenido una estancia agradable.**	Eymoass tayneedoa oonah aystahnthyah ahgrahdhahblay.
Is there a reduction for children?	**¿Hay algún descuento para los niños?**	Igh ahlgoon dayskwayntoa pahrah loass neenyoass?
I think there's a mistake in the bill.	**Creo que hay una equivocación en la factura.**	Krehoa kay igh oonah aykeebhoa-kahthyon ayn lah fahktoorah
This bill is wrong.	**Esta factura está equivocada.**	Aystah fahktoorah aystah aykeebhoa-kahdhah.
Can I have my luggage brought down?	**¿Me pueden bajar el equipaje?**	May pwaydhayn bahkahr ayl aykeepahkhay?
Can you make the bill in my firm's name?	**¿Pueden hacer la factura a nombre de mi empresa?**	Pwaydhayn ahthayr lah fahktoora ah noambray day mee aymprayssah?
I'm coming back in February.	**Vuelvo en febrero.**	Bwaylboa ayn fehbrehroa.
Can I reserve a room for that date?	**¿Puedo reservar una habitación para esa fecha?**	Pwaydhoa rayssayr-bahr oonah ahbhee-tahthyon pahrah aysah faychah.
Can you have my luggage taken to a taxi?	**¿Pueden llevarme el equipaje a un taxi?**	Pwaydhayn lyaybhahrmay ayl aykeepahkhay ah oon tahksee.
Will you accept a check?	**¿Aceptan cheques?**	Ahthayptahn chaykays?
I don't have enough cash.	**No tengo bastante dinero en efectivo.**	Noa tayngoa bahstahntay deenayroa ayn ayfaykteeboa.

| Are all the extras included in the bill? | **¿Están incluidos en la factura todos los extras?** | Aystahn eenklooeedhoass ayn lah fhactoorah toadhoass loass ayhkstrahs? |
| Can you send any messages to this address? | **¿Puede mandar cualquier mensaje a esta dirección?** | Pwayday mahndahr kwahlkyar maynssahkay ah aystah deerehkthyon? |

Vocabulary - Vocabulario

to accept	**aceptar**	ahthaayptahr
pleasant	**agradable**	ahgrahdhahblay
enough	**bastante**	bahstahntay
bill	**cuenta**	kwayntah
cheque	**cheque**	chaykay
address	**dirección**	deerehkthyon
cash	**en efectivo**	ayn ayfaykteeboa
send	**enviar**	aynbeeahr
mistake	**equivocación**	aykeebhoakahthyon
wrong	**equivocado**	aykeebhoakahdhoa
stay	**estancia**	aystahnthyah
date	**fecha**	faychah
tax	**impuestos**	eempwaystoass
included	**incluido**	eenklooeedhoah
to leave	**irse**	eersay
ready	**listo, preparado**	leestoa, praypahrahdoa
tomorrow morning	**mañana por la mañana**	mahnyahnah porr lah mahnyahnah
to think	**pensar**	paynsahr
reduction	**reducción**	raydookthyon
coming back	**vuelvo**	bwaylboa

Money
Dinero

Where's the nearest exchange office?	**¿Dónde está la oficina de cambio más cercana?**	Doanday aystah lah oafeetheenah day kahmbyoa mahss thayrkahnah?
Is there a bank near here?	**¿Hay un banco cerca de aquí?**	Igh oon bahnkoa thayrkah day ahkee?
Can I change ten thousand pesetas into pounds?	**¿Puedo cambiar diez mil pesetas en libras?**	Pwaydhoa kahmbyahr dyayth meel payssaytahss ayn leebrahss?
Will you take a cheque?	**¿Aceptan cheques?**	Ahthaypthan chaykays?
Where can I cash this cheque?	**¿Dónde puedo cobrar este cheque?**	Doanday pwaydoa koabrahr aystay chaykay?
Will you take my credit card?	**¿Aceptan mi tarjeta de crédito?**	Ahthayptahn mee tahrkhaytah day kraydeetoa?
What's the rate of exchange?	**¿A cómo está el cambio?**	Ah koamoa aystah ayl kahmbyoa?
I want to open an account.	**Quiero abrir una cuenta.**	Kyayroa ahbreer oonah kwayntah.
May I change this into pesetas?	**¿Podría cambiar esto en pesetas?**	Poadreeah kambyar aystoa ayn payssaytahss?

Can I cash these trevellers' cheques?	**¿Puedo cobrar estos cheques de viaje?**	Pwaydoa koabrahr aystoas chaykays day byahkyay?
Go to the cashier.	**Vaya al cajero.**	Bahyah ahl kahkayroa.
Where do I sign?	**¿Dónde firmo?**	Doanday feermoa?
Sign here, please.	**Firme aquí, por favor.**	Feermay ahkee, porr fahbhor.

Vocabulary - Vocabulario

to change	**cambiar**	kahmbyar
exchange	**cambio**	kahmbyoa
rate of exchange	**el cambio**	ayl kahmbyoa
checks	**cheques**	chaykays
to cash	**cobrar**	koabrahr
how much?	**¿cuánto?**	kwahntoa?
account	**cuenta**	kwayntah
dollars	**dólares**	doalahrayss
the nearest	**el más cercano**	ayl mahss thayrkahnoa
pounds	**libras**	leebrahss
credit card	**tarjeta de crédito**	tahrkhaytah day kraydeetoa

Travel(l)ing.
Viajando.

Travel(l)ing by taxi - Viajando en taxi

Where's the taxi rank?	**¿Dónde está la parada de taxis?**	Doanday aystah lah pahrahdhah day tahksee?
I want to take a taxi.	**Quiero coger un taxi.**	Kyayroa koahkayr oon tahksee.
Are you free?	**¿Está usted libre?**	Aystah oosthaydh leebray?
Take me to this hotel.	**Lléveme a este hotel.**	Lyaybhaymay ah aystay oatehl
Take us to the station.	**Llévenos a la estación.**	Lyaybhaynoass ah lah aystahthyon.
Can you hurry?	**¿Puede darse prisa?**	Pwaydhay dahrssay preessah?
We are late.	**Vamos tarde.**	Bahmoass tahrday.
Wait here, please.	**Espere aquí, por favor.**	Ayspayray ahkee, porr fahbhor.
Stop here.	**Pare aquí.**	Pahray ahkee
Where can I get a taxi?	**¿Dónde puedo conseguir un taxi?**	Doanday pwaydoa koansehgeehr oon tahksee?
Get me a taxi, please.	**Consígame un taxi, por favor.**	Koanseehgahmay oon tahksee, porr fabhor.
What's the fare to...?	**¿Cuánto vale ir a ...?**	Kwahntoa bahlay eehr ah...?
Turn left.	**Gire a la izquierda.**	Kheeray ah lah eethkyayrdah.
Can you help me with the bags?	**¿Puede ayudarme con las bolsas?**	Pwayday ahyoodharmay kon lahs bolsahss?
Go straight ahead.	**Vaya todo derecho.**	Bahyah toadhoa dayraychoa.
Turn right at the corner.	**Gire a la derecha en la esquina.**	Kheeray ah lah dayraychah ayn lah ayskeenah.

How much do you charge per hour/ per day?	**¿Cuánto cobran por hora / por día?**	Kwahntoa koabrahn porr oarah/porr deeah?
How much would it cost to go to...?	**¿Cuánto costaría ir a ...?**	Kwahntoa koastahreeah eer ah..?
It's too much.	**Es demasiado.**	Ayss daymahssyahdoa.

Vocabulary - Vocabulario

the change	**el cambio**	ehl kahmbyoa
near	**cerca**	thayrkah
to take	**coger**	koahkayrr
how much?	**¿cuánto?**	kwahntoa?
right	**derecha**	dayraychah
adress	**dirección**	deerehkthyon
wait	**espere**	ayspayray
turn	**gire**	kheeray
keep	**guarde**	gooahrday
left	**izquierda**	eethkyayrdah
rank	**parada**	pahrahdah
far	**lejos**	layhkhoss
free	**libre**	leebray
to carry	**llevar**	lyebahr
more slowly	**más despacio**	mahss dayspahthyoa
faster	**más rápido**	mahss rahpeedhoa
stop here	**pare aquí**	pahray ahkee
hurry	**prisa**	preesah
late	**tarde**	tahrday
taxi	**taxi**	tahksee

Travel(l)ing by air - Viajando en avión

At what time are we taking off?	**¿A qué hora despegamos?**	Ah kay oarah dayspaygahmoass?
At what time are we leaving?	**¿A qué hora salimos?**	Ah kay oarah sahleemoass?
When is the next plane?	**¿Cuándo es el próximo avión?**	Kwahndoa ayss ayl prokseemoa ahbyon?
When do I have to check in?	**¿Cuándo debo presentarme?**	Kwahndoa dayboa praysayntahrmay?

Can I change my ticket?	**¿Puedo cambiar el billete?**	Pwaydoa kahmbyar ayl beelyaytay?
When do we arrive?	**¿Cuándo llegamos?**	Kwahndoa lyaygahmoass?
At what time are we landing?	**¿A qué hora aterrizamos?**	Ah kay oarah ahtayrreethahmoasss?
Is there a flight to New York?	**¿Hay un vuelo a Nueva York?**	Igh oon bwayloa ah Nwaybah Yoark?
What's the flight number?	**¿Cuál es el número del vuelo?**	Kwahl ayss ayl noomayroa day bwayloa?
I want to book two seats.	**Quiero reservar dos asientos.**	Kyayroa rayssayrbahr doss assyayntoass
How much more will it cost?	**¿Cuánto más me costará?**	Kwahntoa mahss may koahstahrah?
I want an open ticket.	**Quiero un billete abierto.**	Kyayroa oon beelyaytay ahbeeayrtoa
Please, cancel my reservation.	**Cancele mi reserva, por favor.**	Kahnthayhlay mee rayssayrbah, porr fahbhor.
Is there a bus or a train to the city center?	**¿Hay algún autobús o tren al centro de la ciudad?**	Igh ahlgoon owtoabhooss oa trayn ahl thayntroa day lah thyoodhahdh?
When does it leave?	**¿Cuándo sale?**	Kwahndoa sahlay?
Where's the airline office?	**¿Dónde está la oficina de las líneas aéreas?**	Doanday aystah lah oafeetheenah day lahs leenayahs ahayrayahs
Stewardess, can you bring me a whisky?	**Azafata, ¿puede traerme un whisky?**	Ahthahfahtah, pwayday trahayrmay oon weeskee?

Vocabulary - Vocabulario

open	**abierto**	ahbeeayhrtoa
height	**altura**	ahltoorah
seats	**asientos**	ahssyayntoass
landing	**aterrizando**	ahtayrreethahndoa
plane	**avión**	ahbhyon
cancel	**cancelar/anular**	kahnthaylahr/ahnoolahr

taking off	**despegando**	dayspaygahndoa
airline	**líneas aéreas**	leenayahs ahayrayahs
check in	**presentarse**	praysayntahrsay
reservation	**reserva**	rayssayrbah
to book	**reservar**	rayssayrbahr
to leave	**salir**	sahleer
to take	**tardar**	tahrdahr
flying	**volando**	boahlahndoa
flight	**vuelo**	bwayloa

Travel(l)ing by train - Viajando en tren

What time does the train leave?	**¿A qué hora sale el tren?**	Ah kay oarah sahlay ayl trayn?
Which platform does it leave from?	**¿De qué andén sale?**	Day kay ahndayn sahlay?
What time does it arrive?	**¿A qué hora llega?**	Ah kay oorah lyaygah?
When does the train from Zaragoza get in?	**¿Cuándo llega el tren de Zaragoza?**	Kwahndoa lyaygah ayl trayn day Thahrahgoathah?
At which platform?	**¿En qué andén?**	Ayn kay ahndayn?
Does the train stop at Burgos?	**¿Para el tren en Burgos?**	Pahrah ayl trayn ayn Boorgoass?
Do I have to change?	**¿Tengo que cambiar?**	Tayngoa kay kahmbyahr?
Is there a connection to Valencia?	**¿Hay alguna combinación a Valencia?**	Igh ahlgoonah koambeenahthyon ah Vahlayntheeah?
Where's the railway station?	**¿Dónde está la estación del ferrocarril?**	Doanday aysta lah aystahthyon dayl fehrrokahrreel?
Where's the ticket office?	**¿Dónde está la taquilla?**	Doanday aysta lah tahkeelyah?
I want a seat in a non-smoker.	**Quiero un asiento en un compartimento de no fumadores.**	Kyayroa oon ahssyayntoa ayn oon kompahrteemayntoa day noa foomahdhorayss

I want a seat in a smoking compartment.	**Quiero un asiento en un compartimento de fumadores.**	Kyayroa oon ahssyayntoa ayn oon kompahrtee-mayntoa day foomahdhorayss.
Is there a restaurant car on this train?	**¿Hay un coche restaurante en este tren?**	Igh oon koachay raystowrahntay ayn aystay trayn?
When is the next train to Madrid?	**¿Cuándo es el próximo tren a Madrid?**	Kwahndoa ayss ayl prokseemoa trayn ah Mahdreedh.
Is there a through train to Sevilla?	**¿Hay algún tren directo a Sevilla?**	Igh ahlgoon trayn deerehktoa ah Saybeeleeah?
Is this seat free?	**¿Está libre este asiento?**	Aystah leebray aystay ahssyayntoa?
This seat is taken.	**Este asiento está ocupado.**	Aystay ahssyayntoa aystah oakoopahdhoa
Where's the sleeping car?	**¿Dónde está el coche-cama?**	Doanday aystah ayl koachay kahmah?
Which is my sleeper?	**¿Cuál es mi litera?**	Kwahl ayss mee leetayrah?
How long do we stop here?	**¿Cuánto tiempo paramos aquí?**	Kwahntoa teehaympoa pahrahmoass ahkee?
The heating is very low/high.	**La calefacción está muy baja / alta.**	Lah kahlayfahkthyon aystah mwee bahkha/ahltah

Vocabulary - Vocabulario

platform	**andén**	ahndayn
seat	**asiento**	ahssyantoa
heating	**calefacción**	kahlayfahkthyon
sleeping car	**coche-cama**	koachay kahmah
restaurant car	**coche restaurante**	koachay raystowrahntay
compartment	**compartimento**	kompahrteemayntoa
baggage	**equipaje**	aykeepahkay
register	**facturar**	fahktoorahr
sleeper	**litera**	leetayrah
later	**más tarde**	mahss tahrday
earlier	**más temprano**	mahss taymprahnoa

porter	**mozo**	moathoa
ticket collector	**revisor**	raybeesoar
ticket office	**taquilla**	tahkeelyah
train	**tren**	trayn
through train	**tren directo**	trayn deerehktoa
window	**ventanilla**	bayntahneelyah

Travel(l)ing by bus - Viajando en autobús

Where's the bus/ coach station?	**¿Dónde está la estación de autobuses.**	Doanday aysta lah aystahthyon day owtoabhoossayss?
Does the bus stop here?	**¿Para el autobús aquí?**	Pahrah ayl owtoaboos ahkee?
The bus to the Center stops over there.	**El autobús al Centro para allí.**	Ayl owtoabooss ahl thayntroa pahra ahlyee.
Which bus goes to the station?	**¿Qué autobús va a la estación?**	Kay owtoaboos bah ah lah aystahthyon?
Where can I get a bus to the beach?	**¿Dónde puedo coger un autobús a la playa?**	Doanday pwaydhoa coakhayrr oon owtoaboos ah lah plahyah?
There are buses every 20 minutes.	**Hay autobuses cada veinte minutos.**	Igh owtoaboossayss kahdah bayntay meenootoass.
What's the fare?	**¿Cuánto vale el billete?**	Kwahntoa bahlay ayl beelyaytay?
Is there a sightsee- ing tour?	**¿Hay algún recorrido turístico?**	Igh ahlgoon rayhkoarreedhoa tooreesteekoa?
How long does it take?	**¿Cuánto se tarda?**	Kwahntoa say tahrdah?
When does the coach leave?	**¿Cuándo sale el autocar?**	Kwahndoa sahlay ayl owtoakahr?
What time does the coach get to Cambridge?	**¿A qué hora llega el autocar a Cambridge?**	Ah kay oorah lyay- gah ayl owtoakahr ah Kaymbreech?
What stops does it make?	**¿Qué paradas hace?**	Kay pahrahdahss ahthay?

This is a request stop.	**Esta es una parada discrecional.**	Aysta ayss oonah pahrahdah deeskraythyonahl.
Does this bus go to the beach?	**¿Va este autobús a la playa?**	Bah aystay owtoaboos ah lah plahyah?
Where can I leave my luggage?	**¿Dónde dejo el equipaje**	Doanday dayhkoa ayl aykeepahkhay?
Is there a toilet on the coach?	**¿Hay servicios en el autocar?**	Igh sehrbeethyoass ayn ayl owtoakahr?
Can I smoke on the coach?	**¿Puedo fumar en el autocar?**	Pwaydhoa foomahr ayn ayl owtoakahr?
Does this bus stop at our hotel?	**¿Para este autobús en nuestro hotel?**	Pahrah aystay owtoaboss ayn nwasystroa oatehl?

Vocabulary - Vocabulario

to get off	**apearse**	ahpayahrsay
every	**cada**	kahdah
how often?	**¿cada cuánto?**	kahdah kwahntoa?
excursion	**excursión**	aykskoorsyon
it runs	**hace el recorrido**	ahthay ayl rehkorreedhoa
sightseeing	**haciendo turismo**	ahtheeayndoa tooreesmoa
fare	**importe del billete**	eempoartay dayl beelyaytay
journey	**viaje**	byahkhay
trip	**viaje**	byahkhay
tour	**vuelta**	bwayltah

Hiring a car - Alquilando un coche

I want to hire a car.	**Quiero alquilar un auto.**	Kyayro ahlkeelahr oon owtoa.
How much does it cost per hour/day?	**¿Cuánto cuesta por hora/día?**	Kwahntoa kwaystah porr oarah/deeah?
Do you want my driving licence?	**¿Quiere mi permiso de conducir?**	Kyayray mee pehrmeessoa day kondootheer?
Is patrol included?	**¿Está la gasolina incluida?**	Aystah lah gahssoaleenah eenklooeedhah?

Is mileage included?	¿Está incluido el kilometraje?	Aystah eenklooeedhoa ayl keeloamaytrahkhay?
I want full insurance.	Quiero seguro a todo riesgo.	Kyayroa saygooroa ah toadhoa ryaysgoa.
Do you have any special rates?	¿Tienen tarifas especiales?	Tyaynayn tahreefahss ayspaythyahlayss?
Is there a midweek rate?	¿Hay una tarifa para días de labor?	Igh oonah tahreefah pahrah deeahs day lahboar?
Are there any weekend arrangements?	¿Hay algún arreglo para el fin de semana?	Igh ahlgoon ahrraygloa pahrah ayl feen day saymahnah?
Can I have a big car, please?	¿Me da un coche grande, por favor?	May dah oon koachay grahnday, porr fahbhor?
What's the charge?	¿Cuánto cobran?	Kwahntoa koabrahn?
Can I leave the car somewhere in Santander?	¿Puedo dejar el coche en algún sitio en Santander?	Pwaydhoa daykhar ayl koachay ayn ahlgoon seeteeoa ayn Sahntahndayr?
Can you give me the address of your agent in...?	¿Me da la dirección de su agente en...?	May dah lah deerehkthyon day soo ahkhayntay ayn...?
Do you have an office in...?	¿Tienen oficina en...?	Tyanay oafeetheenah ayn...?
I want a large automatic car.	Quiero un coche automático grande.	Kyayroa oon koachay owtoamahteekoa grahnday.
Could you show me how to work the lights?	¿Podría enseñarme cómo funcionan las luces?	Poadreeah aynsay-nyahrmay koamoa foontheeoanahn lahs loothays?
Show me how the reverse gear works.	Enséñeme cómo funciona la marcha atrás.	Aynsaynyaymay koamoa foontheeoanah lah mahrchah ahtrahs.
Where's the horn?	¿Dónde está la bocina?	Doanday aysta lah boatheenah?
I don't like this car.	No me gusta este coche.	Noa may goostah aystay koachay.
Can I have another car?	¿Me da otro coche?	May dah oatroa koachay?
I want a bigger/ smaller car.	Quiero un coche más grande/más pequeño.	Kyayroa oon koachay mahss grahnday/ mahss paykaynyoa.

Vocabulary - Vocabulario

accelerator	**acelerador**	ahthaylayrahdoar
hire, rent	**alquilar**	ahlkeelahr
automatic	**automático**	owtoamahteekoa
horn	**bocina**	boatheenah
charge	**cobrar**	koabrahr
deposit	**depósito**	dayppoaseetoa
return	**devolver**	dayboalbayr
brakes	**frenos**	fraynoass
to work	**funcionar**	foonthyonahr
large, big	**grande**	grahnday
mileage	**kilometraje**	keeloamaytrahkhay
windscreen wipers	**limpia parabrisas**	leempyah pahrahbreessahss
lights	**luces**	loothays
reverse gear	**marcha atrás**	mahrchah ahtrahs
windscreen	**parabrisas**	pahrahbreessahss
small, little	**pequeño**	paykaynyoa
driving licence	**permiso de conducir**	pehrmeessoa day kondootheer
insurance	**seguro**	saygooroa
wheel	**volante**	boalahntay

Driving - Conduciendo

How far is the nearest petrol station?	**¿Qué distancia hay a la próxima gasolinera?**	Kay deestahnthyah igh ah lah proakseemah gahssoaleenayrah
Is there a garage near here?	**¿Hay un garaje cerca de aquí?**	Igh oon gahrahkhay thehrkah day ahkee?
Do you have a road map?	**¿Tiene algún mapa de carreteras?**	Tyaynay ahlgoon mahpah day cahrraytayrahss?
Fill it up please.	**Lleno, por favor.**	Lyaynoa, porr fabhor.
Clean the windscreen.	**Limpie el parabrisas.**	Leempyay ayl pahrahbreessahss.
Change the oil.	**Cambie el aceite.**	Kahmbyay ayl ahthaytay.
Check the battery.	**Compruebe la batería.**	Koamprwaybay lah bahtayreeah.

What's the speed limit?	**¿Cuál es el límite de velocidad?**	Kwahl ays ayl leemeetay day bayloatheedahdh?
Where is there a car park?	**¿Dónde hay un aparcamiento?**	Doanday igh oon ahpahrkahmyayntoa?
I've run out of petrol.	**Me he quedado sin gasolina.**	May eh kaydahdoa seen gahssoaleenah.
I've had a breakdown.	**He tenido una avería.**	Eh tayneedoa oonah ahbayreeah.
Can you send a mechanic?	**¿Puede mandar un mecánico?**	Pwaydhay mahndahr oon maykahneekoa?
How long will you be?	**¿Cuánto tardará?**	Kwahntoa tahrdahrah?
What time does the garage close?	**¿A qué hora cierra el garaje?**	Ah kay oarah thyayrrah ayl gahrahkhay.
Where are the toilets?	**¿Dónde están los servicios?**	Doanday aystahn loass sayrbeethyoass.
Have you a breakdown service?	**¿Hay servicio de averías?**	Igh sayrbeethyoa day ahbayreeahs.
Can you give me a lift to a telephone?	**¿Me lleva hasta un teléfono?**	May lyaybhah ahstah oon taylayfoanoa?
My car won't start.	**No me arranca el coche.**	Noa may ahrrahnkah ayl koachay.
I have a flat tyre.	**Tengo pinchazo.**	Tayngoa peenchahthoa.
Where are you?	**¿Dónde está usted?**	Doanday aystah oostaydh?
Where's your car?	**¿Dónde está su coche?**	Doanday aystah soo koachay?

Vocabulary - Vocabulario

oil	**aceite**	ahthaytay
motorway	**autopista**	owtoapeesstah
road	**carretera**	kahrraytayrah
check	**comprobar**	koamproabahr
diversion	**desvío**	daysbeeoa
one way street	**dirección única**	deerehkthyon ooneekah
garage	**garaje**	gohrahkhay
petrol station	**gasolinera**	gahssoaleenayrah
wash	**lavar**	lahbahr
keep right	**mantener la derecha**	mahntaynayr lah dayraychah

pedestrians	**peatones**	payahtoanays
danger	**peligro**	payleegroa
tyre pressure	**presión de los neumáticos**	prayssyon day loass nayomahteekoass
no parking	**prohibido aparcar**	proaeebeedoa ahpahrkahr
no entry	**prohibida la entrada**	proaeebeedah lah ayntrahdah
fill	**rellenar**	raylaynahr
toilets	**servicios**	sayrbeethyoass
speed	**velocidad**	bayloatheedahdh

At the garage - En el garaje

My car won't start.	**No me arranca el coche.**	Noa may ahrrahnkah ayl koachay.
The engine is firing badly.	**El motor funciona mal.**	Ayl moator foontheeoanah mahl.
The battery is flat.	**La batería está descargada.**	Lah bahtayreeah aystah dayskahrgahdah.
I've lost my car keys.	**He perdido las llaves del coche.**	Eh payrdeedoa lahs lyahbays dayl koachay.
Can you repair it?	**¿Puede arreglarlo?**	Pwayday ahrrayglahrloa?
How much will it cost?	**¿Cuánto costará?**	Kwahntoa koastahrah?
When will the car be ready?	**¿Cuándo estará listo el coche?**	Kwahndoa aystahrah leestoa ayl koachay?
Can you rapair the flat tyre?	**¿Puede arreglar la rueda pincha-da?**	Pwaydhay ahrrayglar lah rwaydhah peenchahdah.
We haven't got spares.	**No tenemos recambios.**	Noa taynaymoass raykahmbyoass.
There's something wrong with...	**Hay algo que no va bien en...**	Igh ahlgoa kay noa bah beeayn ayn.
the car.	**el auto.**	ayl owtoa.
the brakes.	**los frenos.**	loass fraynoass.
the steering wheel.	**el volante.**	boahlahntay.
the lights.	**las luces.**	lahs loothays.
the clutch.	**el embrague.**	ayl aymbrahgay.
the engine.	**el motor.**	ayl moator.
the battery.	**la batería.**	lah bahtayreeah.

There's a smell of petrol.	**Huele a gasolina.**	waylay ah gahssoaleenah.
The engine is overheating.	**El motor se calienta.**	Ayl moator say kahlyayntah.
It's smoking.	**Está sacando humo.**	Aystah sahkahndoa oomoa.
Can you repair it temporarily?	**¿Puede arreglarlo de momento?**	Pwaydhay ahrrayglahrloa day moamayntoa?
You need a new oil pump.	**Necesita una bomba de aceite nueva.**	Naythayseetah oonah boambah day ahthaytay nwaybah.

Vocabulary - Vocabulario

accelerator	**acelerador**	ahthaylayrahdoar
anti-freeze	**anti-congelante**	ahntee-konkhlaylahntay
battery	**batería**	bahtayreeah
bulb	**bombilla**	boambeelyah
plug	**bujía**	bookheeah
gearbox	**caja de cambios**	kahkhah day kahmbyoass
bonnet	**capot**	kahpoat
cylinder	**cilindro**	ceeleendroa
tank	**depósito**	daypoaseetoa
distributor	**distribuidor**	deestreebweedoar
clutch	**embrague**	aymbrahgay
brakes	**frenos**	fraynoass
jack	**gato**	gahtoa
indicator	**intermitente**	eentayrmeetayntay
lights	**luces**	loothays
trunk	**maletero**	mahlaytayroa
number plate	**matrícula**	mahtreekoolah
engine	**motor**	moatoar
door	**puerta**	pwayrtah
spares	**recambios**	raykahmbyoass
spare wheel	**rueda de repuesto**	rwaydah day raypwaystoa
window	**ventanilla**	bayntahneelyah
steering wheel	**volante**	boahlahntay

Sightseeing
**Visita
turística**

Where's the Tourist Office/Information Centre?	¿Dónde está la Oficina de Turismo / el Centro de Información?	Doanday aystah lah oafeetheenah day tooreesmoa/ayl thayntroa day eenformahthyon?
What are the main points of interest?	¿Dónde están los puntos principales de interés?	Doanday aystahn loass poontoass preentheepahlays day eentayrayss?
Where can I get information?	¿Dónde puedo conseguir información?	Doanday pwaydhoa konsaygyr eenformahthyon?
Is there a good sightseeing tour?	¿Hay algún recorrido turístico bueno?	Igh ahlgoon rehkorredhoa tooreesteekoa bwaynoa?
Are there any popular excursions?	Hay alguna excursión popular?	Igh ahlgoonah ayskskoorsyon poapoolahr?
Is there a map of the places to visit?	¿Hay algún mapa de los lugares que visitar?	Igh ahlgoon mahpah day loass loogahrays kay beeseetahr?
Do you have any guidebooks?	¿Tiene alguna guía?	Tyaynay ahlgoonah geeah?
Is there an excursion to the castle?	¿Hay alguna excursión al castillo?	Igh ahlgoonah ayskoorsyon ahl kahsteelyoa?
Is the gallery open on Sundays?	¿Está abierta la galería los domingos?	Aystah ahbhyayrtah lah gahlayreeah loass doameengoass?

When does it open?	**¿Cuándo abre?**	Kwahndoa ahbray?
How much is the entrance fee?	**¿Cuánto es la entrada?**	Kwahntoa ays lah ayntrahdah?
Can I buy a catalogue?	**¿Puedo comprar un catálogo?**	Pwaydoa komprahr oon kahtahloagoa?
Is it all right to take photographs?	**¿Se pueden sacar fotos?**	Say pwaydhayn sahkahr foatoass?
Are there reductions for children?	**¿Hay descuento para niños?**	Igh dayskwayntoa pahrah neenyoass?
Where do I buy a ticket?	**¿Dónde compro la entrada?**	Doanday komproa lah ayntrahdah?
Is admission free?	**¿Es gratis la entrada?**	Ays grahtees lah ayntrahdah?
Is there a catholic/anglican church near here?	**¿Hay alguna iglesia católica/anglicana cerca de aquí?**	Igh ahlgoonah eeglayssyah kahtoaleekah/ahngleekahnah thayrkah day ahkee?
Is there a synagogue/mosque in this town?	**¿Hay alguna sinagoga/mezquita en esta ciudad?**	Igh ahlgoonah seenahgoagah/mayth-keetah ayn aystah thyoodhahdh?
At what time is mass?	**¿A qué hora es la misa?**	Ah kay oorah ays lah meessah?
I'd like to see the priest/vicar/rabbi.	**Quisiera ver al sacerdote/vicario/rabino.**	Keessyayrah bayr ahl sahthehrdoatay/beekaryoa/rahbheenoa.
What's on at the cinema/theatre tonight?	**¿Qué echan en el cine/teatro esta noche?**	Kay aychahn ayn ay theenay/tayahtroa aystah noachay?
Can you recommend a revue/musical?	**¿Puede recomendarme una revista/un musical?**	Pwaydhay rakoamayndahrmay oonah rehbheestah/oon moosseekahl?
What time does the performance begin?	**¿A qué hora empieza la función?**	Ah kay oorah aympyathah lah foonthyon?
Who is directing the orchestra?	**¿Quién dirige la orquesta?**	Kyayn deereekhay lah oarkaystah?

Can I have two seats for the matinée?	¿Me da dos entradas para la matinal?	May dah doss ayn-trahdhahs pahrah lah mahteenahl?
I want a seat in the stalls.	Quiero una butaca.	Kyayroa oonah bootahkah.
How much are the tickets in the circle?	¿Cuánto valen las entradas de anfiteatro?	Kwahntoa bahlayn lahs ayntrahdhahs day ahnfeetayahtroa?
May I have a programme, please?	¿Me da un programa, por favor?	May dah oon proagrahmah, porr fahbhor?
Where's the Opera House/Concert Hall?	¿Dónde está la Casa de la Ópera/Sala de Conciertos?	Doanday aystah la kahsah day lah oapayrah/sahlah day konthyayrtoass?
What's on at the opera tonight?	¿Qué hay en la ópera esta noche?	Kay igh ayn lah oapayrah aystah noachay?
Is there a concert?	¿Hay un concierto?	Igh oon konthyayrtoa?
Who's singing?	¿Quién canta?	Kyayn kahntah?
Which orchestra is playing?	¿Qué orquesta toca?	Kay oarkaystah toakah?
Who is the conductor?	¿Quién es el director?	Kyayn ayss ayl deerayktoar?
Where can we go dancing?	¿A dónde podemos ir a bailar?	Ah doanday poadhaymoass eer ah bighlahr?
Is there a discoteque in town?	¿Hay una discoteca en la ciudad?	Igh oonah deeskoataykah ayn lah thyoodhahdh?
May I have this dance?	¿Me concede este baile?	May konthaydhay aystay bighlay?
Would you like to dance?	¿Le gustaría bailar?	Lay goostahryah bighlahr?
Is there a jazz club here?	¿Hay algún club de jazz aquí?	Igh ahlgoon kloob day yass ahkee?
Which is the best disco in town?	¿Cuál es la mejor discoteca de la ciudad?	Kwahl ays lah mehkor deeskoataykah day lah thyoodhahdh?

Where's the nearest tennis court / golf club?	**Dónde está la pista de tenis /club de golf más cercano?**	Doanday aystah lah peestah day tayneess / kloob day goalf mahss thehrkahnoa?
What's the charge per game / per hour?	**¿Cuánto cuesta por partido /por hora?**	Kwahntoa kwaystah porr pahrteedhoa/ porr oarah?
Where can we go swimming?	**¿Adónde podemos ir a nadar?**	Ah doanday poadhaymoass eer ah nahdhahr?
Is there a swimming pool/skating rink?	**¿Hay alguna pisci-na/pista de patina-je?**	Igh ahlgoonah peestheenah/ peestah day pahteenahkhay?
I'd like to go cross-country skiing/to a football match.	**Me gustaría ir a hacer esquí de fondo/a un partido de fútbol.**	May goostahreeah eerr ah ahthayr ayskee day foandoa/ ah oon pahrteedhoa day footbol
Where is the race course?	**¿Dónde está el hipódromo?**	Donday aystah ayl eepoadroamoa?
Who is the jockey?	**¿Quién es el jockey?**	Kyayn ays ayl yoakayy?
What are the odds on this horse?	**¿Cómo están las apuestas en este caballo?**	Koamoa aystahn lahs ahpwaystahs ayn aystay kahbhahlyoa?

Vocabulary - Vocabulario

admission	**admisión**	ahdmeessyon
circle	**anfiteatro**	ahnfeetayahtroa
odds	**apuestas**	ahpwaystahs
to dance	**bailar**	bighlahr
dancing	**baile**	bighlay
a dance	**un baile**	oon bighlay
stall	**butaca**	bootahkah
castle	**castillo**	kahsteelyoa
catalogue	**catálogo**	kahtahloagoa
catholic	**católico**	kahtoaleekoa

golf club	**club de golf**	kloob day goalf
jazz club	**club de jazz**	kloob day yass
charge	**cobrar**	koabrahr
buy	**comprar**	komprahr
reduction	**descuento**	dayskwayntoa
conductor	**director**	deerayktoar
directing	**dirigiendo**	deereekhyayndoa
discoteque, disco	**discoteca**	deeskoataykah
entrance fee	**entrada**	ayntrahdah
skiing	**esquiar**	ayskyahr
all right	**está bien**	aystah byayn
excursion	**excursión**	aykskoorsyon
photographs	**fotografías**	foatoagrahpheeahss
performance	**función**	foonthyon
gallery	**galería**	gahlayreeah
free	**gratis**	grahtees
guidebook	**guía**	geeah
race course	**hipódromo**	eepoadroamoa
jockey	**hockey**	yoakayy
church	**iglesia**	eeglayssyah
information	**información**	eenformahthyon
interest	**interés**	eentayrayss
game	**juego**	khwaygoa
places	**lugares**	loogahrayss
matinée	**matinal**	mahteenahl
mosque	**mezquita**	maythkeetah
mass	**misa**	meesah
musical	**musical**	mooseekahl
swimming	**natación**	nahtahthyon
orchestra	**orquesta**	oarkaystah
football match	**partido de fútbol**	pahrteedhoa day footbol
swimming pool	**piscina**	peestheenah

skating rink	**pista de patinaje**	peestah day pahteenahkhay
tennis court	**pista de tenis**	peestah day tayneess
main points	**principales puntos**	preentheepahlayss poontoass
rabbi	**rabino**	rahbheenoa
revue	**revista**	rehbheestah
priest	**sacerdote**	sahthehrdoatay
sinagogue	**sinagoga**	seenahgoagah
tourist	**turista**	tooreestah
vicar	**vicario**	beekahryo
sightseeing	**visita turística**	beeseetah tooreesteekoa
visit	**visitar**	beeseetahr
tour	**vuelta**	bwayltah

What time is it?
¿Qué hora es?

What time do you leave work?	**¿A qué hora sales del trabajo?**	Ah kay oarah sahlayss dayl trahbhakhoa?
What time does the Post Office close/open?	**¿A qué hora cierra/abre Correos?**	Ah kay oarah ahbray/theeayrrah korrehoass?
Can you tell me the time, please?	**¿Puede decirme la hora, por favor?**	Pwayday daytheermay lah oarah, porr fahbhor?
It is ten o'clock.	**Son las diez.**	Son lahs dyayth
It is half past eleven.	**Son las once y media.**	Son lahs onthay ee maydhyah
At a quarter past five.	**A las cinco y cuarto.**	Ah lahs theenkoa ee kwahrtoa
What time was it when she came?	**¿Qué hora era cuando vino?**	Kay oarah ayrah kwahndoa beenoa?
At what time did it happen?	**¿A qué hora sucedió?**	Ah kay oarah soothaydeeoa?
It was very late.	**Era muy tarde.**	Ayrah mwee tahrday
It is very early.	**Es muy temprano.**	Ayss mwee taymprahnoa
It was about midday/midnight.	**Era sobre mediodía/medianoche.**	Ayrah soabray maydhyoadheeah/maydhyahnoachay
What time is the train/coach leaving?	**¿A qué hora sale el tren/autocar?**	Ah kay oarah sahlay ayl trayn/owtoakahr?
What time does the plane take off?	**¿A qué hora despega el avión?**	Ah kay oarah dayspaygah ayl ahbhyon?
What time are we arriving?	**¿A qué hora llegamos?**	Ah kay oarah lyaygahmoass?
The train is leaving in five minutes.	**El tren sale dentro de cinco minutos.**	Ayl trayn sahlay dayntroa day theenkoa meenootoas.

The plane is taking off at ten to six.	**El avión despega a las seis menos diez.**	Ayl ahbhyon dayspaygah ah lahs sayss maynoass dyayth.
We are landing in ten minutes.	**Aterrizamos dentro de diez minutos.**	Athayrreethahmoass dayntroa day dyayth meenootoass.
The train is arriving on time.	**El tren llega puntual.**	Ayl trayn lyaygah poontooahl.
What time do the shops open?	**¿A qué hora abren las tiendas?**	Ah kay oarah ahbrayn lahs tyayndahs?
They open at nine o'clock.	**Abren a las nueve.**	Ahbrayn ah lahs nwaybhay.
What time do supermarkets close here?	**¿A qué hora cierran los supermercados aquí?**	Ah kay oarah thyeyrrahn loass soopayrmayr-kahdoass ahkee?
What are your opening times?	**¿Cuáles son sus horas de apertura?**	Kwahlays son soos oarahs day ahpayrtoorah?
Today we are closing at six thirty.	**Hoy cerramos a las seis treinta.**	Oy thayrrahmoass ah lahs sayss trayntah.

Vocabulary - Vocabulario

open	**abre**	ahbray
opening	**apertura**	ahpayrtoorah
land on time	**aterrizamos puntual**	ahtayrreethahmoass poontooahl
close	**cierra**	thyayrrah
lunch	**comida**	koameedhah
post office	**correos**	korrehoass
tell me	**decirme**	daytheerme
breakfast	**desayuno**	dayssahyoonoa
takes off	**despega**	dayspaygah
midnight	**medianoche**	maydhyahnoachay
midday	**mediodía**	maydhyoadheeah
leaves	**sale**	sahlay
happened	**sucedió**	soothaydeeoa
late	**tarde**	tahrday
early	**temprano**	taymprahnoa
shops	**tiendas**	tyayndahs
came	**vino**	beenoa

Asking the way
Preguntando el camino

Excuse me, where's the monument?	**Perdone, ¿dónde está el monumento.**	Payrdoanay, doanday aystah ayl moanoomayntoa?
Where's the National Theatre, please?	**¿Dónde está el Teatro Nacional, por favor?**	Doanday aystah ayl tayahtroa nahtheeoanahl, porr fahbhor?
Can you tell me the way to the harbor/cathedral/Town Hall?	**¿Puede indicarme el camino al puerto / la catedral / el ayuntamiento?**	Pwaydhay eendeekahrmay ayl kahmeenoa ahl pwayrtoa/lah kahtaydrahl/ayl ahyoontahmyayntoa?
Where's the tourist information centre, please?	**¿Dónde está la Información de Turismo, por favor?**	Doanday aystah lah eenformahthyon day tooreesmoa, porr fahbhor?
How far is it?	**¿A qué distancia está?**	Ah kay deestahntheeah aystah?
How can I go there?	**¿Cómo puedo ir allí?**	Koamoa pwaydhoa eer ahlyee?
Can you tell me the way?	**¿Puede decirme el camino?**	Pwaydhay daytheermay ayl kahmeenoa?
Can you show it to me on the map?	**¿Me lo enseña en el mapa?**	May loa aynsaynyah ayn ayl mahpah?
Could you show me the way to the castle, please?	**¿Podría enseñarme el camino al castillo, por favor?**	Poadreeah aynsaynyahrmay ayl kahmeenoa ahl kahsteelyoa, porr fahbhor?

How can we go to the fortress?	**¿Cómo podemos ir a la fortaleza?**	Koamoa poadhaymoass eer ah lah fortahlaytah?
I'm lost. Where am I?	**Ando perdido. ¿Dónde estoy?**	Ahndoa payrdeedhoa. Doanday aystay?
Can you tell me on the map where we are?	**¿Podría indicarme en el mapa dónde estamos?**	Poadreeah een-deekahrmay ayn ayl mahpah doanday aystahmoass?
This is Constitution Square, but where is it on the map?	**Esta es la Plaza de la Constitución, ¿pero dónde está en el mapa?**	Aystah ayss lah plahthah day lah konsteetoothyon, payroa doanday aystah ayn ayl mahpah?
Which is the best way to go to the City Centre?	**¿Cuál es la mejor forma de ir al Centro de la Ciudad?**	Kwahl ayss lah meh-khor formah day eer ahl thayntroa day lah thyoodhahdh?
Can we drive up to the castle?	**¿Podemos ir en coche hasta el castillo?**	Poadaymoass eer ayn koachay ahstah ayl kahsteelyoa?
Can I drive along this street?	**¿Puedo ir en coche por esta calle?**	Pwaydhoa eer ayn koachay porr aystah kahlyay?
Is there a car park in the City Centre?	**¿Hay un aparcamiento en el centro de la ciudad?**	Igh oon ahpahrkah-myayntoa ayn ayl thayntroa day lah thyoodhahdh?
What's the best way to drive out of town?	**¿Cuál es la mejor manera de salir en coche de la ciudad?**	Kwahl ayss lah mehkhor mahnayrah day sahleer ayn koachay day lah thyoodhahdh?
Take the second turning on the left and go on for two hundred meters.	**Coja la segunda bocacalle a la izquierda y siga unos doscientos metros.**	Koakha lah saygoondah boakahkahlyay ah lah eethkyayrdah ee seegah oonoass dosthyayntoass maytroass.

Take the third turning on the right and walk for about a hundred meters. You'll come to a cinema. Turn left there.	Coja la tercera bocacalle a la derecha y camine unos cien metros. Llegará a un cine. Gire a la izquierda allí.	Koakhah lah tehrthayrah boakahkahlyay ah lah dayraychah ee kahmeenay oonoass thyayn maytroass. Lyaygahrah ah oon theenay. Kheeray ah lah eethkyayrdah ahlyee.
Walk along this avenue until you come to the National Theatre. Turn left there and go on for five hundred meters.	Camine por esta avenida hasta que llegue al Teatro Nacional. Allí gire a la izquierda y siga unos quinientos metros.	Kahmeenay porr aystah ahbhayneedah ahstah kay lyaygay ahl tayahtroa nahtheeonal. Ahlyee kheeray ah lah eethkyayrdah ee seegah oonoass keenyayntoass maytroass.
Follow this road until you come to the traffic lights. Turn right and drive for about four or five hundred meters. You'll come to a church on the right.	Siga por esta carretera hasta que llegue a los semáforos. Gire a la derecha y siga conduciendo unos cuatrocientos o quinientos metros. Verá una iglesia a la derecha.	Seegah porr aystah kahrraytayrah ahstah kay lyaygay ah loass saymahfoaroass. Kheeray ah lah dayraychah ee seegah kondoothyayndoa oonahs kwahtroa thyayntoass oa keenyayntoass maytroass. Bayrah oonah eeglayssyah ah lah dayraychah.

Vocabulary - Vocabulario

parking	aparcamiento	ahpahrkahmyayntoa
Town Hall	ayuntamiento	ahyoontahmyayntoa
turning	bocacalle	boakahkahlyay
street	calle	kahlyay
walk	camine	kahmeenay

way	**camino**	kahmeenoa
road	**carretera**	kahrraytayrah
castle	**castillo**	kahsteelyoa
cathedral	**catedral**	kahtaydrahl
take	**coja**	koakhah
tell me	**decirme**	daytheermay
right	**derecha**	dayraychah
distance	**distancia**	deestahntheeah
show me	**enseñarme**	aynsaynyahrmay
way	**forma**	formah
fortress	**fortaleza**	fortahlaythah
turn	**gire**	kheeray
church	**iglesia**	eeglayssyah
show me	**indicarme**	eendeekahrmay
show us	**indicarnos**	eendeekahrnoass
drive	**ir en coche**	eer ayn koachay
left	**izquierda**	eethkyayrdah
way	**manera**	mahnayrah
map	**mapa**	mahpah
better	**mejor**	mehkhor
monument	**monumento**	moanoomayntoa
lost	**perdido**	payrdeedhoa
excuse me	**perdone**	payrdoanay
I can	**puedo**	pwaydhoa
port	**puerto**	pwayrtoa
traffic lights	**semáforos**	saymahfoaroass
go on	**siga**	seegah

Making a phone call
Haciendo una llamada

Operator, I'd like to make a phone call.	**Telefonista, quisiera hacer una llamada telefónica.**	Taylayfoaneestah, keessyayrah ahthayr oonah lyahmahdah taylayfoaneekah
I'd like to speak to Paris, but I don't know the code number.	**Quisiera hablar con París, pero no sé el prefijo.**	Keessyayrah ahblahr kon Pahrees, payroa noa say ayl prayfeekhoa
Can I make a phone call to London from here?	**¿Puedo llamar a Londres desde aquí?**	Pwaydhoa lyahmahr ah Loandrayss daysday ahkee?
A long distance call to the U.S.A.	**Una conferencia a los Estados Unidos.**	Oonah konfayraynthya ah loass Aystahdhoass Ooneedhoass
I'd like to make a phone call to New York, please.	**Me gustaría hacer una llamada a Nueva York, por favor.**	May goostahryah ahthar oonah lyahmahdhah ah Nooaybah Yoar, porr fahbhor.
A long distance collect call to Washington.	**Una conferencia a cobro revertido a Washington.**	Oonah konfayraynthya ah koabroa raybhayr- teedhoa ah Washington.
The number is engaged.	**El número está comunicando.**	Ayl noomayroa aystah komooneekahndhoa.
The line is over-loaded.	**La línea está sobrecargada.**	Lah leenayah aystah soabraykahrgahdhah.
Try again later.	**Pruebe otra vez más tarde.**	Prwaybhay ootrah bayth mahss tahrday.
I'll get you through to Sr. Rodriguez.	**Le pongo con el Sr. Rodríguez.**	Lay poangoa kon ayl saynyor Roadreegueth.
What's your room number?	**¿Cuál es el número de su habitación?**	Kwahl ays ayl noomayroa day soo ahbheetahthyon?

You can speak now.	**Pueden hablar ahora.**	Pwaydhayn ahblahr ahoarah.
Can I speak to Sr. Gomez, please?	**¿Puedo hablar con el Sr. Gómez, por favor?**	Pwaydhoa ahblahr kon ayl saynyor Goamayth, porr fahbhor.
With the export department, please.	**Con el departamento de exportación, por favor.**	Kon ayl daypahrtahmaynto day aykspoartahthyon, porr fahbhor.
With Sr. Perez, the manager, please.	**Con el Sr. Pérez, el director, por favor.**	Kon ayl saynyor Payrayth, ayl deereeayktoar, porr fahbhor.
Sr. Benito is on the other line.	**El Sr. Benito está en la otra línea.**	Ayl saynyor Bayneetoah aystah ayn lah oatrah leenayah
Mr. Cruz is out. He won't be back until this afternoon.	**El Sr. Cruz ha salido. No volverá hasta esta tarde.**	Ayl seynyor Crooth ah sahleedoa. Noa boalbayrah ahstah aystah tahrday.
Srta. Alcain is in a meeting. Can you call again in half an hour?	**La Srta. Alcain está en una reunión. ¿Puede llamar dentro de media hora?**	Lah saynyoareetah Alkine aystah ayn oonah rayoonyon. Pwaydhay lyahmahr dayntroa day maydhyah oorah?
There's no answer at Sr. Lucas's office.	**No responden en la oficina del Sr. Lucas.**	Noa rayspoandayn ayn lah oafeetheenah dayl saynyor Lookahs.
Mr Mendez will call you back in a few minutes.	**El Sr. Méndez le llamará a usted dentro de unos minutos.**	Ayl saynyor Mayndayth lay lyahmahrah ah oostaydh dayntroa day oonoass meenootoass.
Srta. Julia is not in. Can I give her a message?	**La Srta Julia no está. ¿Puedo darle un mensaje?**	Lah saynyoareetah Hooleeah noa aystah. Pwaydhoa dahrlay oon maynsahkhay?
Sr. Alvarez has a visitor. He'll call you back in half an hour.	**El Sr. Álvarez está con una visita. Él les llamará dentro de media hora.**	Ayl saynyor Albahrayth aystah kon oonah beeseetah. Ayl lays lyahmahrah dayntroa day maydhyah oarah.

Please tell him that Mr. Rossini has called.	**Dígale por favor que el Sr. Rossini ha llamado.**	Deegahlay porr fahbhor kay ayl saynyor Rossini ah lyahmahdo.
Tell Sr. Valverde that I am at the Hilton Hotel.	**Dígale al Sr. Valverde que estoy en el hotel Hilton.**	Deegahlay ahl saynyor Balbayrday kay aystoay ayn ayl oatehl Hilton.
Can you tell Sr. Rosser that I'll be expecting his call?	**¿Puede decirle al Sr. Rosser que estaré esperando su llamada?**	Pwaydhay daytheerlay ahl saynyor Roassayr kay aystahray ayspayrahndoa soo lyahmahdah.
Tell Srta. Nuria that I'll call again in half an hour.	**Dígale a la Srta Nuria que volveré a llamar dentro de media hora.**	Deegahlay ah lah saynyoareetah Nooreeah kay boalbayray ah lyahmahr dayntroa day maydhyah oarah.

Vocabulary - Vocabulario

collect call	**cobro revertido**	koabroa raybhayrrteedhoa
engaged	**comunicando**	komooneekahndhoa
long distance call	**conferencia**	konfayraynthya
again	**de nuevo**	day nwayboa
expecting	**esperando**	ayspayrahndoa
export	**exportación**	aykspoartahthyon
out	**fuera**	fwayrah
phone call	**llamada telefónica**	lyahmahdah taylayfoaneekah
later	**más tarde**	mahss tahrday
message	**mensaje**	maynsahkhay
few	**pocos**	poakoass
get you through to	**poner con**	ponayr kon
code number	**prefijo**	prayfeekhoa
try	**probar, intentar**	probahr, eentayntahr
answer	**respuesta**	rayspwaystah
meeting	**reunión**	rayoonyon
overloaded	**sobrecargado**	soabraykahrgahdhoa
operator	**telefonista**	taylayfoaneestah
visitor	**visita**	beeseetah
be back	**volver**	boalbayr

At the police station
En la comisaría

I want to report a theft.	**Quiero informar de un robo.**	Kyeroa eenformahr day oon roabhoa.
My passport was stolen.	**Me han robado el pasaporte.**	May ahn roabhahdhoa ayl pahssahportay.
Somebody has stolen my bag.	**Alguien me ha robado el bolso.**	Ahlgyayn may ah roabhahdhoa ayl boalsoa.
My case was stolen in the airport.	**Me han robado la maleta en el aeropuerto.**	May ahn roabhahdhoa lah mahlaytah ayn ayl ahehroapwayrtoa.
I've lost my bag.	**Se me ha perdido el bolso.**	Say may ah pehrdeedhoa ayl boalsoa.
I've lost my wallet.	**Se me ha perdido la cartera.**	Say may ah pehrdeedhoa lah kahrtayrah.
We've lost our dog.	**Se nos ha perdido el perro.**	Say noass ah pehrdeedhoa ayl payrroa.
My car has disappeared.	**Mi coche ha desaparecido.**	Mee koachay ah daysahpahraytheedhoa.
Where's the nearest police station?	**¿Dónde está la comisaría más cercana?**	Doanday aystah lah koameessahreeah mahss therkahnah?
I'm looking for a policeman.	**Estoy buscando un policía.**	Aystay booskahndoa oon poaleetheeah.
Can you describe the bag?	**¿Puede describirme el bolso?**	Pwaydhay dayskreebeermay ayl boalsoa?
What colo(u)r is it?	**¿De qué color es?**	Day kay koaloar ayss?
What does it look like?	**¿Qué aspecto tiene?**	Kay ahspayktoa tyaynay?

What make is it?	**¿De qué marca es?**	Day kay mahrkah ayss?
What breed is it?	**¿De qué raza es?**	Day kay rahthah ayss?
It's brown and square.	**Es marrón y cuadrado.**	Ayss mahrron ee kwahdrahdoa.
My wife's passport is inside.	**El pasaporte de mi mujer está dentro.**	Ayl pahssahportay day mee mookher aystah dayntroa.
It's round and black.	**Es redonda y negra.**	Ayss raydoandah ee nehgrah.
It's a brown leather case.	**Es una maleta de cuero marrón.**	Ayss oonah mahlaytah day kwayroa mahrron.
My driving licence is inside.	**Mi permiso de conducir está dentro.**	Mee pehrmeessoa day kondootheer aystah dayntroa.
What did you see, sir?	**¿Qué ha visto, señor?**	Kay ah beestoa, saynyor?
I saw the accident.	**He visto el acciden- te.**	Eh beestoa ayl ahktheedhayntay.
It didn't stop at the traffic lights.	**No ha parado en el semáforo.**	Noa ah pahrahdoa ayn ayl saymahfoaroah.
The little boy ran across the road.	**El niño atravesó la carretera corriendo.**	Ayl neenyoa ahtrah- baysoa lah kahrray- tayrah korryayndoa.
When I looked, the man was already under the car.	**Cuando miré, el hombre estaba ya debajo del coche.**	Kwahndhoa meeray, ayl oambray aystahbah yah daybhahkhoa dayl koachay.
I heard a noise but I didn't see any- thing.	**Oí un ruido pero no vi nada.**	Oy oon rweedoa payroa noa bee nahdah.
I heard the crash, but I didn't see what happened.	**Oí el choque pero no vi lo que pasó.**	Oy ayl choakay payroa noa bee loa kay pahsoa.
I couldn't see any- thing from where I was.	**No pude ver nada desde donde yo estaba.**	Noa poodhay bayr nahdah daysday doanday yoa aystahbah.

Vocabulary - Vocabulario

accident	**accidente**	ahktheedhayntay
airport	**aeropuerto**	ahehroapwayrtoa
ran across	**atravesó corriendo**	ahtrahbaysoa korryayndoa
bag	**bolso**	boalsoa
looking for	**buscando**	booskahndoa
wallet	**cartera**	kahrtayrah
crash	**choque**	choakay
police station	**comisaría**	koameessahreeah
square	**cuadrado**	kwahdrahdoa
under	**debajo**	daybhahkhoa
inside	**dentro**	dayntroa
disappeared	**desaparecido**	daysahpahraytheedoa
describe	**describir**	dayskreebeer
wife	**esposa**	ayspoasah
to report	**informar**	eenformahr
what	**lo que**	loa kay
case	**maleta**	mahlaytah
make	**marca**	mahrkah
brown	**marrón**	mahrron
nearest	**más cercana**	mahss therkahnah
looked	**miré**	meeray
didn't stop	**no paró**	noa pahroa
I heard	**oí**	oy
passport	**pasaporte**	pahssahportay
dog	**perro**	payrroa
look like	**qué aspecto**	kay ahspayktoa
breed	**raza**	rahthah
stolen	**robado**	roabahdhoa
theft	**robo**	roabhoa
noise	**ruido**	rweedoa
traffic lights	**semáforo**	saymahfoaroah
happened	**sucedió**	soothaydyoa
I saw	**vi**	bee
already	**ya**	yah

At the post office
En correos

Where's the nearest post office?	**¿Dónde está la oficina de correos más cercana?**	Doanday aystah lah oafeetheenah day korrehoass mahss thehrkahnah?
Where's the main post office?	**¿Dónde está la oficina de correos principal?**	Doanday aystah lah oafeetheenah day korreoahs preentheepahl?
Where's the letter-box?	**¿Dónde está el buzón?**	Doanday aystah ayl boothon?
What time does the post office open?	**¿A qué hora abre correos?**	Ah kay oarah ahbray korrehoass?
Which counter do I go to for stamps/ telegrams/money orders?	**¿A qué mostrador voy a por sellos/ telegramas/giros postales?**	Ah kay moastrahdhor boy ah porr saylyoass/ taylaygrahmahs/ kheeroass postahlays?
Telegrams at that counter.	**Los telegramas en ese mostrador.**	Loass taylaygrahmahs ayn aysay moastrahdhor
Stamps are sold at that counter.	**Los sellos se venden en aquel mostrador.**	Loass saylyoass say bayndayn ayn ahkayl moastrahdhor
There's a letter-box at the corner of the street.	**Hay un buzón en la esquina de la calle.**	Igh oon boothon ayn lah ayskeenah day lah kahlyay
Can I have some stamps, please?	**¿Me da unos sellos, por favor?**	May dah oonoass saylyoass, porr fahbhor?
Give me ten 40-peseta. stamps, please.	**Deme 10 sellos de 40 pesetas, por favor.**	Daymay dyayth say- lyoass day kwahrayntah paysaytahs, porr fahbhor.

Can I have three 25-peseta stamps, please?	**¿Me da 3 sellos de 25 pesetas, por favor?**	May dah trayss saylyoass day baynteetheenkoa paysaytahs, porr fahbhor.
How many do you want, sir?	**¿Cuántos quiere, señor?**	Kwahntoass kyayray, saynyor?
Here you are, madam. Ten 20-peseta stamps. 200 pesetas, please.	**Aquí tiene, señora, 10 sellos de veinte pesetas. 200 pesetas, por favor.**	Ahkee tyaynay, saynyoarah, dyayth saylyoass day bayntay paysaytahs. Dosstheeayntahs paysaytahs, porr fahbhor.
How much is it to send a letter surface mail?	**¿Cuánto vale enviar una carta por correo ordinario?**	Kwahntoa bahlay aynbeeahr oonah kahrtah porr korrehoa oardeenahryo?
I want to send this letter express.	**Quiero enviar esta carta urgente.**	Kyayroa aynbeeahr aystah kahrtah oorkhayntay.
I want to register this letter.	**Quiero mandar esta carta certificada.**	Kyayroa mahndahr aystah kahrtah thayrteefeekahdah.
What's the postage for a letter to Europe.	**¿Cuánto es el franqueo de una carta a Europa?**	Kwahntoa ayss ayl frahnkayoa day oonah kahrtah ah Ayooroapah?
Which window do I go to for stamps?	**¿A qué ventanilla voy a por sellos?**	Ah kay bayntahneelyah boy ah porr saylyoass?
Airmail express, please. How much will it be?	**Por avión, urgente, por favor. ¿Cuánto será?**	Por ahbhyon, oorkayntay, porr fabhor, kwahntoa sayrah?
Registered mail, please.	**Correo certificado, por favor.**	Korreoa thayrteefeekahdoa, porr fahbhor.
Postage for surface mail is *550 pts*.	**El franqueo para el correo ordinario es 550 pesetas.**	Ayl frahnkayoa pahrah ayl korrehoa oardeenahryo ayss keeneeayntahs theenkwayntah paysaytahs.

If you want to register the letter fill in this form.	**Si quiere certificar la carta rellene este impreso.**	See kyayray thayrteefeekahr lah kahrtah raylyaynay aystay eemprayssoa.
The postage to England, airmail is *150 pts.*	**El franqueo a Inglaterra por avión es 150 pesetas.**	Ayl frahnkayoa ah Eenglahtayrrah porr ahbhyon ayss theeayntoh theenkwentah.
You can buy stamps at all these windows.	**Se pueden comprar sellos en todas esas ventanillas.**	Say pwaydhayn komprarhr saylyoass ayn toadahs aysahs bayntahneelyahs
I want to send a parcel, express, please.	**Quiero mandar un paquete urgente, por favor.**	Kyayroa mahndahr oon pahkaytay oorkhayntay, porr fabhor.
Can I send this parcel to England?	**¿Puedo enviar este paquete a Inglaterra?**	Pwaydhoa aynbeeahr oon pahkaytay ah Eenglatayrrah?
Do I need to fill in a customs declaration?	**¿Tengo que rellenar un impreso de aduanas?**	Tayngoa kay raylyaynahr oon eemprayssoa day ahdwahnahs?
I want to register a parcel.	**Quiero mandar un paquete certificado.**	Kyayroa mahndahr oon pahkaytay thayrteefeekahdhoa.
I'd like to send a telegram, please.	**Quisiera enviar un telegrama, por favor.**	Keessyayrah aynbeeahr oon taylaygrahmah, porr fahbhor.
How much does it cost per word?	**¿Cuánto cuesta por palabra?**	Kwahntoa kwaystah porr pahlahbra?
May I have a form for a telegram?	**¿Me da un impreso para un telegrama?**	May dah oon eemprayssoa pahrah oon taylaygrahmah?
How long will a cable to London take?	**¿Cuánto tardará un cable a Londres?**	Kwahntoa tahrdahrah oon kahblay ah Lohndrays?
I want to send a cable, it's rather urgent.	**Quiero enviar un cable, es muy urgente.**	Kyayroa aynbeehr oon kahblay, ayss mwee oorkhayntay.

Vocabulary - Vocabulario

customs	**aduanas**	ahdwahnahs
letter-box	**buzón**	boothon
cable	**cable**	kahblay
letter	**carta**	kahrtah
registered	**certificado**	thayrteefeekahdoa
surface mail	**correo ordinario**	korrehoa oardeenahryo
express	**correo urgente**	korrehoa oorkhayntay
post office	**correos**	korrehoass
how long	**cuánto tiempo**	kwahntoa tyaympoa
declaration	**declaración**	daykhlahrahthyon
corner	**esquina**	ayskeenah
postage	**franqueo**	frahnkayoa
money order	**giro postal**	kheeroa postahl
form	**impreso**	eemprayssoa
nearest	**más cercano**	mahss therkahnoa
may I have?	**¿me da...?**	may dah...?
counter	**mostrador**	moastrahdhor
rather	**muy**	mwee
urgent	**urgente**	oorkhayntay
word	**palabra**	pahlahbrah
parcel	**paquete**	pahkaytay
airmail	**por avión**	porr ahbhyon
main	**principal**	preentheepahl
I'd like	**quisiera**	keesyayrah
fill in	**rellenar**	raylyaynahr
stamps	**sellos**	saylyoass
telegrams	**telegramas**	taylaygrahmahs
window	**ventanilla**	bayntahneelyah

At the restaurant
En el restaurante

Where can we find a good restaurant?	**¿Dónde podemos encontrar un buen restaurante?**	Doanday poadhaymoass aynkontrahr oon bwayn raystowrahntay?
Is there a typical restaurant around here?	**¿Hay algún restaurante típico por aquí?**	Igh ahlgoon raystowrahntay teepeekoa porr ahkee?
Can you suggest a cheap restaurant?	**¿Puede recomendarnos un restaurante barato?**	Pwaydhay raykoamayndahrnoass oon raystowrahntay bahrahtoa?
A table for two, please.	**Una mesa para dos, por favor.**	Oonah mayssah pahrah doss, porr fahbhor.
I prefer the one by the window.	**Prefiero la que está junto a la ventana.**	Prayfeeayroa lah kay aystah khoontoa ah lah behntahnah.
Is there a table on the terrace?	**¿Hay una mesa en la terraza?**	Igh oonah mayssah ayn lah tayrrahthah?
A table in the corner, please.	**Una mesa en el rincón, por favor.**	Oonah mayssah ayn ayl reenkon, porr fahbhor.
Can I have the menu?	**¿Me da el menú?**	May dah ayl maynoo?
I'd like to book a table for tonight, please.	**Quisiera reservar una mesa para esta noche, por favor.**	Keessyayrah rayssayrbahr oonah mayssah pahrah aystah noachay, porr fahbhor.
What time do you start serving dinner?	**¿A qué hora empiezan a servir las cenas?**	Ah kay oorah aympyaythahn ah sehrbeer lahs thaynahs?
Do you have a table for eight?	**¿Tiene mesa para ocho?**	Tyaynay mayssah pahrah oachoa?

Are we too early?	**¿Venimos demasiado temprano?**	Bayneemoass daymahssyahdhoa taymprahnoa?
I'd like to book a table for Saturday night.	**Quisiera reservar una mesa para el sábado por la noche.**	Keessyayrah rayssayrbahr oonah mayssah pahrah ayl sahbhadhoa porr lah noachay.
Will nine o'clock be all right?	**¿Estará bien a las nueve?**	Aystahrah byayn ah lahs nwaybhay?
I want to reserve a table for tonight.	**Quiero reservar una mesa para esta noche.**	Kyayroa rayssayrbahr oonah mayssah pahrah aystah noachay.
We'll be here at eight thirty.	**Estaremos aquí a las ocho y media.**	Aystahraymoass ahkee ah lahs oachoa ee maydhyah
Can I have a table for this evening?	**¿Me da una mesa para esta noche?**	May dah oonah mayssah pahrah aystah noachay?
What time can we come?	**¿A qué hora venimos?**	Ah kay oarah bayneemoass?
We'll wait in the bar.	**Esperaremos en el bar.**	Ayspayrahraymoass ayn ayl bahr.
Bring us the menu and two glasses of wine.	**Tráiganos el menú y dos vasos de vino.**	Trighahnoass ayl maynoo ee doss bahssoass day beenoa.
Will you have a table free soon?	**¿Tendrá alguna mesa libre pronto?**	Tayndrah ahlgoonah mayssah leebray proantoa?
Do you serve dinners before 8 p.m.?	**¿Sirven cenas antes de las ocho?**	Seerbayn thaynahs ahntays day lahs oachoa?

Vocabulary - Vocabulario

evening	**atardecer**	ahtahrdaythayr
cheap	**barato**	bahrahtoa
dinners	**cenas**	thaynahs
too early	**demasiado temprano**	daymahssyahdhoa taymprahnoa

to start	**empezar**	aympaythahr
to find	**encontrar**	aynkontrahr
to wait	**esperar**	ayspayrahr
tonight	**esta noche**	aystah noachay
by the window	**junto a la ventana**	khoontoa ah lah behntahnah
free	**libres**	leebrays
night	**noche**	noachay
around here	**por aquí**	porr ahkee
soon	**pronto**	proantoa
to book	**reservar**	raysayrbahr
corner	**rincón**	reenkon
to serve	**servir**	sehrbeer
suggest	**sugerir**	sookhayreer
terrace	**terraza**	tayrrahtha
to bring	**traer**	trahayr
glasses	**vasos**	bahssoass
wine	**vino**	beenoa

Ordering breakfast - Pidiendo el desayuno

I want some breakfast, please.	**Quiero desayunar, por favor.**	Kyayroa dayssahyoonahr, porr fahbhor.
Can I have two boiled eggs?	**¿Me da dos huevos duros?**	May dah doss waybhoass dooroass?
An orange juice, please.	**Un zumo de naranja, por favor.**	Oon thoomoa day nahrahnkhah, porr fahbhor.
A glass of grapefruit juice.	**Un vaso de zumo de pomelo.**	Oon bahssoa day thoomoa day poamayloa.
Bacon and eggs.	**Tocineta y huevos.**	Toatheenaytah ee waybhoass.
Two scrambled eggs.	**Dos huevos revueltos.**	Doss waybhoass raybhwayltoass.
A black coffee and a white coffee.	**Un café solo y un café con leche.**	Oon kahfay soaloa ee oon kahfay kon laychay.
A glass of hot milk.	**Un vaso de leche caliente.**	Oon bahssoa day laychay kahlyayntay

A plate of ham and eggs.	**Un plato de jamón con huevos.**	Oon plahtoa day khahmon kon waybhoass.
A boiled egg.	**Un huevo cocido.**	Oon waybhoa koatheedhoa.
soft/medium/hard.	**blando/medio/duro.**	blahndoa / maydeeoa / dooroa.
Can I have some toast with jam?	**¿Me da unas tostadas con mermelada?**	May dah oonahss toastahdhahs kon mehrmaylahdhah?
Some more bread and butter, please.	**Algo más de pan y mantequilla, por favor.**	Ahlgoa mahss day pahn ee mahntaykeelyah, porr fahbhor.
A cup of hot chocolate.	**Una taza de chocolate caliente.**	Oonah tahthah day choakoalahtay kahlyayntay
Caffein-free coffee, please.	**Café descafeinado, por favor.**	Kayfay dayskahfayeenahdhoa, porr fahbhor,
Can I have honey instead of sugar?	**¿Me da miel en vez de azúcar?**	May dah myehl ayn bayth day ahthookahr?
Can we have some tea with milk/lemon?	**¿Nos da té con leche/limón?**	Noass dah tay kon laychay/leemon?
I'll have two fried eggs with bacon.	**Tomaré dos huevos fritos con tocineta.**	Toamahray doss waybhoass kon toatheenaytah.
Can we have champagne and cakes?	**¿Nos da champán con pasteles?**	Noass dah champahn kon pahstaylays?
Do you have a free buffet?	**¿Tienen buffet libre?**	Tyaynayn boafayt leebray?
Can I have some cereal with milk?	**¿Me da unos cereales con leche?**	May dah oonoass thayrayahlayss kon laychay?

Vocabulary - Vocabulario

soft	**blando**	blahndoa
free buffet	**buffet libre**	boofayt leebray
black coffee	**café solo**	kahfay soaloa
white coffee	**café con leche**	kahfay kon laychay

champagne	**champán**	chahmpahn
boiled	**cocido**	koatheedhoa
breakfast	**desayuno**	dayssahyoonoa
caffein-free	**descafeinado**	dayskahfayeenahdhoa
hard	**duro**	dooroa
egg	**huevo**	waybhoa
ham	**jamón**	khahmon
milk	**leche**	laychay
lemon	**limón**	leemon
butter	**mantequilla**	mahntaykeelyah
medium	**medio**	maydeeoa
jam	**mermelada**	mehrmaylahdhah
honey	**miel**	myehl
bread	**pan**	pahn
cakes	**pasteles**	pahstaylayss
grapefruit	**pomelo**	pomayloa
scrambled	**revueltos**	raybhwayltoas
bacon	**tocineta**	toatheenaytah
toast	**tostadas**	toastahdhahss
juice	**zumo**	thoomoa

Ordering dinner - Encargando la comida

I want soup and steak, please.	**Quiero sopa y filete, por favor.**	Kyayroa soapah ee feelaytay
A mixed salad for two.	**Una ensalada mixta para dos.**	Oonah aynsahlahdhah meehkstah pahrah doss.
Can I have trout and ham?	**¿Me trae trucha con jamón?**	May trahhay troochah kon khahmon?
Fish soup for me and asparagus for my wife.	**Sopa de pescado para mí y espárragos para mi mujer.**	Soahpah day payskahdhoa pahrah mee ee aysparrahgoass pahrah mee mookher.
A bottle of red wine and water.	**Una botella de vino tinto y agua.**	Oonah boataylyah day beenoa teentoa ee ahgwah.

A glass of beer and orange juice.	**Un vaso de cerveza y zumo de naranja.**	Oon bahssoa day thayrbhaythah ee thoomoa day nahrahnkhah
Meat for me and fish for my wife.	**Carne para mí y pescado para mi mujer.**	Kahrnay pahrah mee ee payskahdhoa pahrah mee mookhehr.
We'd like some starters, please.	**Quisiéramos unos entremeses, por favor.**	Kessyayrahmoass oonoass ayntraymay-ssayss, porr fahbhor.
What do you recommend?	**¿Qué nos recomiendan?**	Kay noass raykomyayndhah?
Can I have a napkin and another glass, please?	**¿Me trae una servilleta y otro vaso, por favor?**	May trahay oonah sehrbeelyaytah ee oatroa bahssoa, porr fahbhor?
We don't have an ashtray.	**No tenemos cenicero.**	Noa taynaymoass thayneethayroa
Can we smoke in the restaurant?	**¿Podemos fumar en el restaurante?**	Poadaymoass foomahr ayn ayl raystowrahntay?
Do you have the dish of the day?	**¿Tienen el menú del día?**	Tyaynayn ayl maynoo dayl deeah?
Do you have any poultry and game?	**¿Tienen aves y caza?**	Tyaynayn ahbhayss ee kahthah?
I'd like to try the seafood.	**Me gustaría probar el marisco.**	May goostahryah proabahr ayl mahreeskoa.
Do you have cheese?	**¿Tienen queso?**	Tyaynayn kayssoa?
We'd like to have two aperitifs.	**Quisiéramos dos aperitivos.**	Keesyayrahmoass doss ahpayreeteeboass.
What do you have for dessert?	**¿Qué tienen para postre?**	Kay tyaynayn pahrah poastray?
I like this sauce.	**Me gusta esta salsa.**	May goostah aystah sahlsah.
Where's the vinegar and the oil?	**¿Dónde está el vinagre y el aceite?**	Doanday aystah ayl beenahgray ee ayl athaytay?
Can I have the bill, please?	**¿Me da la cuenta, por favor?**	May dah lah kwayntah, porr fahbhor?
Keep the change.	**Guárdese el cambio.**	Gwahrdaysay ayl kahmbyo

Vocabulary - Vocabulario

water	**agua**	ahgwah
waitress	**camarera**	kahmahrayrah
waiter	**camarero**	kahmahrayroa
meat	**carne**	kahrnay
ashtray	**cenicero**	thayneethayroa
beer	**cerveza**	thayrbhaytha
spoon	**cuchara**	koachahrah
knife	**cuchillo**	koocheelyoa
bill	**cuenta**	kwayntah
salad	**ensalada**	aynsahlahdhah
cloakroom	**guardarropa**	gwahrdahrroapah
headwaiter	**maitre**	maytray
table cloth	**mantel**	mahntayl
mustard	**mostaza**	moastahthah
bread	**pan**	pahn
fish	**pescado**	payskahdhoa
saucer	**platillo**	plahteelyoa
plate	**plato**	plahtoa
dessert	**postre**	poastray
salt	**sal**	sahl
sauce	**salsa**	sahlsah
napkin	**servilleta**	sehrbeelyaytah
fork	**tenedor**	taynaydhoar
omelets	**tortillas**	toarteelyahs
glass	**vaso**	bahssoa
wine	**vino**	beenoa

The menu: Starters - El menu: Entremeses

kippered herring	**arenque ahumado**	ahrehnkay ahoomahdhoa
tunny in olive oil	**atún en aceite de oliva**	ahtoon ayn athaytay day oaleebhah
canapés	**canapé**	kahnahpay
lobster cocktail	**cóctel de langosta**	koaktayl day lahngoastah

shellfish cocktail	**cóctel de marisco**	koaktayl day mahreeskoa
croquettes	**croquetas**	kroakaytahs
tomato salad	**ensalada de tomate**	aynsahlahdhah day toamahtay
shrimps	**gambas**	gahmbahss
York ham	**jamón de York**	khakmon day Yoark
oysters	**ostras**	ostrahss
salami	**salchichón**	sahlsheechoan
smoked salmon	**salmón ahumado**	sahlmon ahoomahdoa
smoked trout	**trucha ahumada**	troochah ahoomahdah

Typical Spanish dishes - Platos típicos españoles.

paella Valencian style	**paella valenciana**	pahyelyah valenthianah
hake Basque style	**merluza a la vasca**	mayrloothaah ah lah Bahskah
Asturian fabada	**fabada asturiana**	fahbahdah Ahstooryahanah
stew Madrid style	**cocido madrileño**	kotheedoh Mahdrilenyoh
roast lamb	**cordero asado**	kordayroh assahdoh
Segovian sucking pig	**cochinillo segoviano**	kochinilyoh saygohvyahnoh
codfish	**bacalao**	bahkahlaow
potatoes Rioja style	**patatas a la riojana**	pahtahtahs ah lah reeohahnah
cod in pil pil sauce	**bacalao al pil-pil**	bahkahlahoa ahl pill pill
cod Biscay style	**bacalao a la vizcaina**	bahkahlahoa ah lah beathkynah

Soups - Sopas

chicken consommé	**caldo de gallina**	kahldoa day gahlyeenah
consommé	**consomé**	konsoamay
consommé with sherry	**consomé al jerez**	konsoamay ahl kherayth
cream of spinach soup	**crema de espinacas**	kraymah day ayspeenahkahss
cream of green pea soup	**crema de guisantes**	kraymah day geesahntayss
garlic soup	**sopa de ajo**	soapah day ahkhoa
pupkin soup	**sopa de calabaza**	soapah day kahlahbahthah
onion soup	**sopa de cebolla**	soapah day thayboalyah
a kind of broth	**sopa de cocido**	soapah day koatheedoa
noodle soup	**sopa de fideos**	soapah day feedhayoass
chicken soup	**sopa de gallina**	sopapah day gahlyeenah
aspargus soup	**sopa de espárragos**	soapah day ayspahrrahgoass
seafood soup	**sopa de marisco**	soapah day mahreeskoa
mussel soup	**sopa de mejillones**	soapah day mehkheelyoanayss
fish soup	**sopa de pescado**	soapah day payskahdhoa
oxtail soup	**sopa de rabo de buey**	soapah day rahbhoa day bway
tomato soup	**sopa de tomate**	soapah day toamahtay
vegetable soup	**sopa de verduras**	soapah day bayrdoorahs

Omelets - Tortillas

fried eggs with bacon	**huevos a la americana**	waybhoass ah lah ahmayreekahnah
hard-boiled eggs	**huevos duros**	waybhoass dooroass
poached eggs	**huevos escalfados**	waybhoass ayskahlfahdhoass
ham and eggs	**huevos con jamón**	waybhoass kon khahmon

bacon and eggs	**huevos fritos con tocineta**	waybhoass freetoass kon toatheenaytah
scrambled eggs	**huevos revueltos**	waybhoass raybhwayltoass
artichoke omelet	**tortilla de alcacho-fas**	toarteelyah day ahlkahchoafahss
cod omelet	**tortilla de bacalao**	toarteelyah day bahkahlahoa
onion omelet	**tortilla de cebolla**	toarteelyah day thayboalyah
mushroom omelet	**tortilla de champiñones**	toarteelyah day chahmpeenyoanayss
asparagus omelet	**tortilla de espárra-gos**	toarteelyah day ayspahrrahgoass
plain omelet	**tortilla francesa**	toarteelyah frahnthayssah
ham omelet	**tortilla de jamón**	toarteelyah day khamon
omelet with pota-toes, peas, etc.	**tortilla a la paisana**	toarteelyah ah lah paheessahnah
potato omelet	**tortilla de patatas**	toarteelyah day pahtahtahss
cheese omelet	**tortilla de queso**	toarteelyah day kayssoa
mushroom omelet	**tortilla de setas**	toarteelyah day saytahss
tomato omelet	**tortilla de tomate**	tarteelyah day toamahtay

Fish and seafood - Pescado y marisco

clams	**almejas**	ahlmehkhahss
herring	**arenques**	ahrehnkayss
frog's legs	**ancas de rana**	ahnkahs day rahnah
eel	**anguilas**	ahngeelahs
tunny/tuna	**atún**	ahtoon
tuna-fish with tomato	**atún con tomate**	ahtoon kon toamahtay
cod	**bacalao**	bahkahlahoa
salt cod in tomato sauce	**bacalao en salsa de tomate**	bahkahlahoa ayn sahlsah day toamahtay

sea bream	**besugo**	bayssoogoa
grilled sea bream	**besugo a la parrilla**	bayssoogoa ah lah pahrreelyah
tunny/tuna	**bonito**	boaneetoa
white bait	**boquerones**	boakayroanayss
squid	**calamares**	kahlahmahrayss
mackerel	**caballa**	kahbbahlyah
crab	**cangrejo**	kahngrehkhoa
spider crab	**centollo**	thayntoalyoa
spider-crabs	**centollos**	thayntoalyoass
baby squid	**chipirones**	cheepeeroanayss
prawns	**gambas**	gahmbahss
lobster	**langosta**	lahngoastah
lobster with mayonnaise	**langosta con mayonesa**	lahngoastah kon mahyoanayssah
sole	**lenguado**	layngwahdhoa
fillets of sole	**filetes de lenguado**	feelaytayss day layngwahdhoa
fried sole	**lenguado frito**	layngwahdhoa freetoa
grilled sole	**lenguado a la parrilla**	layngwahdhoa ah lah pahrrelyah
shrimps	**langostinos**	lahngoasteenoass
hake	**merluza**	mayrloothah
fillets of hake	**filetes de merluza**	feelaytayss day mayrloothah
seabass	**mero**	mayroa
mussels	**mejillones**	mahkheelyoanayss
oysters	**ostras**	ostrahss
oysters mornay	**ostras al gratén**	ostrahss ahl grahtayn
perch	**perca**	pehrkah
whiting	**pescadilla**	payskahdheelyah
swordfish	**pez espada**	payth ayspahdhah
octopus	**pulpo**	poolpoa
little shrimps	**quisquillas**	keeskeelyahss
monkfish	**rape**	rahpay
skate	**raya**	rahyah

turbot	**rodaballo**	roadhahbhahlyoa
braised turbot	**rodaballo estofado**	roadhahbhahlyoa aystoafahdhoa
salmon	**salmón**	sahlmon
red mullet	**salmonetes**	sahlmoanaytayss
sardines	**sardinas**	sahrdeenahss
fried sardines	**sardinas fritas**	sahrdeenahss freetahss
cuttlefish	**sepia**	saypeeah
trout	**truchas**	troochahs
rainbow trout	**trucha al arco iris**	troochah ahl ahrkoa eerees
fried trout	**trucha frita**	troochah freetah
trout with ham	**trucha con jamón**	troochah kon khamon
trout meuniere	**trucha a la molinera**	troochah ah lah moaleenayrah

Meats - Carne

meatballs	**albóndigas**	ahlbhoandeegahs
meatballs with tomato	**albóndigas con tomate**	ahlbhoandeegahs kon toamahtay
beefsteak	**bistec**	beestayk
grilled steak	**bistec a la parrilla**	beestayk ah la pahrreelyah
ox	**buey**	bway
ox-tongue	**lengua de buey**	layngwah day bway
oxtail	**rabo de buey**	rahbhoa day bway
kid	**cabrito**	kahbreetoa
tripe	**callos**	kahlyoass
mince meat	**carne picada**	kahrnay peekahdhah
mutton	**cordero**	koardayroa
roast lamb	**asado de cordero**	ahssahdhoa day koardayroa
mutton stew	**estofado de cordero**	aystoafahdhoa day koardayroa
leg of mutton	**pierna de cordero**	pyehrnah day koardayroa
pork	**cerdo**	therdoa

roast pork	**asado de cerdo**	ahssahdhoa day therdoa
pork cutlet	**chuleta de cerdo**	choolaytah day therdoa
breaded pork chop	**chuleta de cerdo empanada**	choolaytah day therdoa aympahnahdah
shoulder of pork	**espaldilla de cerdo**	ayspahdeelyah day therdoa
loin of pork	**solomillo de cerdo**	soaloameelyoa day therdoa
sort of salami	**chorizo**	choareethoa
chops	**chuletas**	choolaytahss
heart	**corazón**	koarahthon
lamb	**cordero**	koardayroa
roast lamb	**asado de cordero**	ahssahdhoa day koardayroa
grilled lamb cutlets	**chuletillas de cordero a la parrilla**	choolayteelyahss day koardayroa ah lah pahreelyah
lamb stew	**estofado de cordero**	aystoafahdhoa day koardayroa
sucking pig	**cochinillo**	koacheeneelyoa
spicy sausages	**embutidos**	aymbooteedhoass
sirloin steak	**entrecote**	ayntraykoat
escalope	**escalope**	ayskahloapay
stew	**estofado**	aystoafahdhoa
black pudding and bean stew	**fabada**	fahbahdah
cold meats	**fiambres**	fyahmbrayss
steak	**filete**	feelaytay
liver	**hígado**	eegahdhoa
ham	**jamón**	khahmon
ham with spinach	**jamón con espinacas**	khahmon kon ayspeenahkahss
tongue	**lengua**	layngwah
young lamb	**lechazo**	laychahthoa
loin of pork	**lomo**	loamoa
sweetbreads	**mollejas**	moalyaykhahss
black pudding	**morcilla**	moartheelyah

At the restaurant - En el restaurante

ossobuco	**ossobuco**	oasoabookoa
feet	**paletilla**	pahlayteelyah
shank	**patas**	pahtahss
leg	**pierna**	pyehrnah
hotpot	**puchero**	poochayroa
pudding	**pudín**	poodeen
kidneys	**riñones**	reenyoanayss
kidneys en brochette	**riñones en brocheta**	reenyoanayss ayn broachaytah
sausages	**salchichas**	sahlcheechahss
brains	**sesos**	sayssoass
tenderloin	**solomillo**	soaloameelyoa
veal	**ternera**	thernayrah
roast veal	**asado de ternera**	ahssahdhoa day tehrnayrah
veal cutlet	**chuleta de ternera**	choolaytah day tehrnayrah
fillet of veal	**filete de ternera**	feelaytah day tehrnayrah
veal stew	**guisado de ternera**	geesahdhoa day tehrnayrah
calf's liver	**hígado de ternera**	eegahdhoa day tehrnayrah
calf's kidney	**riñones de ternera**	reenyoanayss day tehrnayrah
loin of veal	**solomillo de ternera**	soalomeelyoa day tehrnayrah
bacon	**tocino**	toatheenoa
sucking pig	**tostón**	toastoan
beef	**vaca**	bahkah
roast beef	**asado de vaca**	ahssahdhoa day bahkah
rump-steak	**bistec de vaca**	beestayk day bahkah
boiled beef	**cocido de carne de vaca**	koatheedhoa day kahrnay day bahkah
beef stew	**estofado de vaca**	aystoafahdhoa day bahkah

This is how food can be cooked - Así es cómo se cocina la carne

baked	al horno	ahl oarnoa
boiled	hervido	ayrbeedhoa
braised	estofado	aystoafahdhoa
flambéd	flambeado	flahmbayahdhoa
fried	frito	freetoa
grilled	a la parrilla	ah lah pahreelyah
pot roasted	asado en su salsa	ahssahdhoa ayn soo sahlssah
roast	asado	ahssahdhoa
rare	poco hecho	poakoa aychoa
sautéed	salteado	sahltehahdhoa
stewed	estofado	aystoafahdhoa
well-done	muy hecho	mwee aychoa
cured	curado	koorahdhoa
deep fried	muy frito	mwee freetoa
marinated	en escabeche	ayn ayskahbhaychay
poached	escalfado	ayskahlfahdhoa
smoked	ahumado	ahoomahdhoa
steamed	cocido al vapor	koatheedhoa ahl bahpor
double saucepan	baño María	ahl bahnyoa mahreeah
cooked in oil and garlic	al ajillo	ahl ahkheelyoa
barbecued	a la barbacoa	ah lah bahrbahkoa
home-made	casero	kahsayroa
raw	crudo	kroohdhoa
grated	gratinado	grahteenahdoa
fried in batter	rebozado	rayboathahdhoa
meat/fish pie	pastel de carne / pescado	pahstayl day kahrnay/ payskahdhoa

Poultry and game - Aves y carne de caza

woodcock	becada	baykahdhah
woodcock pie	pastel de becada	pahstayl day baykahdhah
capon	capón	kahpon
deer	ciervo,	theeayrboa

quail	**codorniz**	koadoarneeth
roast quails	**codornices asadas**	koadoarneethayss ahssahdhahss
broiled quails	**codornices a la parrilla**	koadoarneethayss ah lah pahrreelyah
quails with grapes	**codornices con uva**	koadoarneethayss kon oobah
rabbit	**conejo**	koanyakhoa
roast rabbit	**conejo asado**	koanaykhoa ahssahdhoa
jugged rabbit	**conejo en salmorejo**	koanaykhoa ayn sahlmoaraykhoa
deer	**corzo**	koarthoa
pheasant	**faisán**	fighssahn
pheasant pie	**pastel de faisán**	pahstayl day fighssahn
breast of pheasant	**pechuga de faisán**	paychoogah day fighsahn
hen	**gallina**	gahlyeenah
goose	**ganso**	gahnsoa
roast goose with apple sauce	**ganso asado con salsa de manzana**	gahnsoa ahssahdhoa kon sahlsah day mahnthahnah
wild boar	**jabalí**	khahbhahlee
roast wild boar	**jabalí asado**	khahbhahlee ahssahdhoa
jugged wild boar	**jabalí en salmorejo**	khahbahlee ayn sahlmouraykhoa
young wild boar	**jabato**	khahbahtoa
hare	**liebre**	lyehbray
roast hare	**liebre asada**	lyehbray ahssahdhah
fillets of hare	**filetes de liebre**	feelaytayss day lyehbray
hare pie	**pastel de liebre**	pahstayl day lyehbray
pigeon	**paloma**	pahloamah
duck	**pato**	pahtoa
roast duck	**pato asado**	pahtoa ahssahdhoa
duckling with oranges	**pato a la naranja**	pahtoa ah lah nahrahnkhah
wild duck with oranges	**pato salvaje a la naranja**	pahtoa sahlbahkhay ah lah nahrahnkhah
turkey	**pavo**	pahbhoa

roast turkey	**pavo asado**	pahbhoa ahssahdhoa
roast stuffed turkey	**pavo asado relleno**	pahbhoa ahssahdhoa raylyaynoa
breast of turkey	**pechuga de pavo**	paychoogah day pahbho
partridge	**perdiz**	pehrdeeth
breast of partridge	**pechuga de perdiz**	paychoogah day pehrdeeth
pigeon	**pichón**	peechoan
chicken	**pollo**	poalyoa
leg of chicken	**muslo de pollo**	moosloa day poalyoa
chicken pie	**pastel de pollo**	pahstayl day poalyoa
breast of chicken	**pechuga de pollo**	paychoogah day poalyoa
roast chicken	**pollo asado**	poalyoa ahssahdhoa
casserole of chicken	**pollo a la cazuela**	poalyoa ah lah cahthwaylah
grilled chicken	**pollo a la parrilla**	poalyoa ah lah pahrreelyah
spring chicken on the spit	**pollo joven a la brasa**	poalyoa khobayn ah lah brahsah
breast	**pechuga**	paychoogah
reindeer	**reno**	raynoa
venison	**venado**	baynahdhoa
escalope of venison	**escalope de venado**	ayskahloapay day baynahdhoa

Vegetables and legumes - Verduras y legumbres

chicory	**achicoria**	ahcheekoaryah
artichoke	**alcachofa**	ahlkahchoafah
beans	**alubias**	ahloobeeahss
celery	**apio**	ahpyoa
aubergine	**berenjena**	bayraynkhaynah
cabbage	**berza**	bayrthah
onion	**cebolla**	thayhboalyah
courgette	**calabacín**	kahlahbhatheen
mushrooms	**champiñones**	champeenyoanayss
parsnips	**chirivías**	cheereebheeahss

Brussels sprouts	**coles de Bruselas**	koalayss day broossaylahss
cauliflower	**coliflor**	koleeflor
asparagus	**espárragos**	ayspahrrahgoass
spinach	**espinacas**	ayspeenahkahss
chickpeas	**garbanzos**	gahrbahnthoass
peas	**guisantes**	geessahntayss
broad bean	**habas**	ahbahss
green beans	**judías verdes**	khoodheeahss behrdayss
lettuce	**lechuga**	laychoogah
lentils	**lentejas**	layntahkhahss
sweet corn	**maíz**	maheeth
potatoes	**patatas**	pahtahtahss
gherkins	**pepinillos**	paypeeneelyoass
cucumber	**pepino**	paypeenoa
parsley	**perejil**	payraykheel
pepper	**pimiento**	peemyayntoa
sweet red peppers	**pimientos morrones**	peemyayntoass moarroanayss
leeks	**puerros**	pwayrroass
radishes	**rábanos**	rahbahnoass
beetroot	**remolacha**	raymoalahchah
cabbage	**repollo**	raypoalyoa
mushrooms	**setas**	saytahss
tomatoes	**tomates**	toamahtayss
truffles	**trufas**	troofahss
carrots	**zanahorias**	thahnahoaryahss

Fruits - Frutas

apricots	**albaricoques**	ahlbahreekoakayss
almonds	**almendras**	ahlmayndrahss
hazelnuts	**avellanas**	ahbhaylyahnahss
peanuts	**cacahuetes**	kahkahwaytayss
chestnuts	**castañas**	kahstahnyahss
cherries	**cerezas**	thayraythahss

cherimoya	**chirimoya**	cheereemoayah
plums	**ciruelas**	theerwaylahss
prunes	**ciruelas pasas**	theerwaylahss pahssahss
coconut	**coco**	koakoa
dates	**dátiles**	dahteelayss
raspberries	**frambuesas**	frahmbwayssahss
strawberries	**fresas**	frayssahss
pomegranates	**granadas**	grahnahdahss
figs	**higos**	eegoass
lime	**lima**	leemah
lemon	**limón**	leemon
tangerine	**mandarina**	mahndahreenah
apple	**manzana**	mahnthahnah
peach	**melocotón**	mayloakoaton
melon	**melón**	maylon
quince	**membrillo**	maynbreelyoa
orange	**naranja**	nahrahnkhah
loquat	**níspero**	neespayroa
walnuts	**nueces**	nwaythayss
raisins	**pasas**	pahssahss
pears	**peras**	pehrahss
pineapple	**piña**	peenyah
banana	**plátano**	plahtahnoa
grapefruit	**pomelo**	poamayloa
watermelon	**sandía**	sahndeeah
grapes	**uvas**	oobhahss

Desserts - Postres

gingerbread	**alajú**	ahlahkhoo
rice pudding	**arroz con leche**	ahrroth kon laychay
sponge cake	**bizcocho**	beethkoachoa
Christmas pudding	**budín de Navidad**	boodeen day nahbeedhahdh

fritters	**buñuelos**	boonywayloass
banana fritters	**buñuelos de plátanos**	boonywayloass day plahtahnoass
applesauce	**compota**	koampoatah
Bavarian choco-late cream	**crema bávara de chocolate**	kraymah bahbrah day chokoalahtay
pancake	**crepe, tortita**	krayp, torteetah
crêpes	**crepes, tortitas**	krayps, torteetahss
caramel pudding	**flan**	flahn
caramel custard	**flan al caramelo**	flahn ahl kahrahmayloa
fritters	**fritos**	freetoass
biscuits	**galletas**	gahlyaytahss
ice-cream coffee chocolate strawberry whipped-cream vanilla yogurt	**helado de café de chocolate, de fresa, de nata, de vainilla, de yogur**	aylahdhoa day kahfay, day choakoalahtay, day frayssah, day nahtah, day bighneelyah, day yoagoor
fruit jelly	**jalea de fruta**	khahlayah day frootahss
marzipan	**mazapán**	mahthahpahn
chocolate mousse	**mousse de chocolate**	mooss day choakoalahtay
whipped cream	**nata batida**	nahtah bahteedah
Spanish custard	**natilla**	nahteelyah
wedding cake	**pastel de boda**	pahstayl day boadah
chocolate cake	**pastel de chocolate**	pahstayl day choakoalahtay
coconut cake	**pastel de coco**	pahstayl day koakoa
cheese cake	**pastel de queso**	pahstayl day kayssoa
apple pie	**pastel de manzana**	pahstayl day mahnthahnah
nut cake	**pastel de nueces**	pahstayl day nwaythayss
banana flambé	**plátanos flameados**	plahtahnoass flahmbayahdoass
doughnuts	**rosquilla**	roaskeelyah
almond cake	**tarta de almendra**	tahrtah day ahlmayndrahss

cherry tart	**tarta de cerezas**	tahrtah day thayraythahss
strawberry cake	**tarta de fresa**	tahrtah day frayssah
fruit tart, fruit pie	**tarta de fruta**	tahrtah day frootah
ice-cream cake	**tarta helada**	tahrtah aylahdhah
apple pie	**tarta de manzana**	tahrtah day mahnthahnah
whisky cake	**tarta al whisky**	tahrtah ahl weeskee
candied egg yolks	**yemas**	yaymahss
trifle	**trifle**	treeflay
chocolate truffles	**trufas de chocolate**	troofahss day choakoalahtay

Drinks - Bebidas

water	**agua**	ahgwah
mineral water	**agua mineral**	ahgwah meenayrahl
coffee	**café**	kahfay
champagne	**cava, champán**	kahbah, chahmpahn
beer	**cerveza**	thayrbhaythah
brandy	**coñac**	koanyahk
lemonade	**gaseosa, limonada**	gahsehoasah, leemoanahdhah
orangeade	**naranjada**	nahrahnkhahdhah
gin	**ginebra**	kheenaybrah
herb tea	**infusiones**	eenfoosyonayss
milk	**leche**	laychay
rum	**ron**	ron
cider	**sidra**	seedrah
tea	**té**	tay
tonic water	**tónica**	toaneekah
white wine	**vino blanco**	beenoa blahnkoa
red wine	**vino tinto**	beenoa teentoa
rosé wine	**vino clarete**	beenoa klahraytay
whisky	**whisky**	weeskee
apple juice	**zumo de manzana**	thoomoa day mahnthahnah

orange juice	**zumo de naranja**	thoomoa day nahrahnkhah
tomato juice	**zumo de tomate**	thoomoa day toamahtay
grape juice	**zumo de uva**	thoomoa day oobhah

Asking for the bill - Pidiendo la cuenta

The bill, please.	**La cuenta, por favor.**	Lah kwayntah, porr fahbhor
Is tax included?	**¿Está incluido el IVA?**	Aystah eenklooeedhoa ayl eebah?
What's this amount for?	**¿De qué es esta cantidad?**	Day kay ayss aystah kahnteedhahdh?
I think there's a mistake.	**Creo que hay una equivocación.**	Krehoa kay igh oonah aykeebhoakahthyon.
Two separate bills, please.	**Dos cuentas separadas, por favor.**	Doss kwayntahss saypahrahdahss, porr fahbhor.
Do you accept travel(l)er's cheques?	**¿Aceptan cheques de viaje?**	Athayptahn chaykayss day byahkhay?
That was a very good meal.	**Ha sido una comida estupenda.**	Ah seedhoa oonah koameedhah aystoopayndah.
We enjoyed the meal, thank you.	**Nos ha gustado mucho la comida, gracias.**	Noss ah goostahdhoa moochoa lah koomeedhah, grahthyass.
Do you accept this credit card?	**¿Aceptan esta tarjeta de crédito?**	Ahthayptahn aystah tahrkhaytah day kraydheetoa?
Keep the change.	**Guarde el cambio.**	Gwahrday ayl kahmbyo.

Age and work of
people.
**La edad y el
trabajo de
la gente.**

How old is that lady?	¿Qué edad tiene esa señora?	Kay aydhahdh tyaynay aysah saynyoarah?
She's forty-five.	Tiene cuarenta y cinco años.	Tyaynay kwahrayntah ee theenkoa ahnyoass.
How old are you?	¿Cuántos años tiene usted?	Kwahntoass ahnyoass tyaynay oostaydh?
I'm twenty.	Tengo veinte años.	Tayngoa bayeentay ahnyoass.
Are you married?	¿Es usted casado?	Ayss oostaydh kahssahdhoa?
Do you have any children?	¿Tiene usted hijos?	Tyaynay oostaydh eekhoass?
How old are they?	¿Cuántos años tienen?	Kwahntoass ahnyoass tyaynayn?
What do they do?	¿En qué trabajan?	Ayn kay trahbahkhahn?
Is Mr Pipe a friend of yours?	¿Es el Sr. Pipe amigo tuyo?	Ayss ayl saynyor Pipe ahmeegoa tooyoah?
How old is he?	¿Cuántos años tiene?	Kwahntoass ahnyoass tyaynay?
Where does he work?	¿Dónde trabaja?	Doanday trahbahkhah?
What do you do?	¿A qué se dedica usted?	Ah kay say daydeekah oostaydh?
I'm a carpenter.	Soy carpintero.	Soay kahrpeentayroa.
I'm a business-man.	Soy empresario.	Soay aympraysahryo.
What does he do?	¿A qué se dedica él?	Ah kay say dahdeekah ayl?
He's a doctor.	Es médico.	Ayss mehdheekoa.
That man is a mechanic.	Ese hombre es mecánico.	Aysay oambray ayss maykahneekoa.

How old is your mother?	¿**Cuántos años tiene tu madre?**	Kwahntoass ahnyoass tyaynay too mahdray.
Our children are 15 and 10.	**Nuestros hijos tienen quince y diez años.**	Nwaystroass eekhoass tyaynayn keenthay ee dyayth ahnyoass.
How old is the baby?	¿**Qué edad tiene el bebé?**	Kay aydhahdh tyaynay ayl baybhay?
He's four months old.	**Tiene cuatro meses.**	Tyaynay kwahtroa mayssayss.
How do you earn your living?	¿**Cómo se gana usted la vida?**	Koamoa say gahnah oostaydh lah beedah?
I'm a dentist?	**Soy dentista.**	Soay daynteestah.
What's your job?	¿**Cuál es su trabajo?**	Kwahl ayss soo trahbahkhoa?
What does your wife do?	¿**A qué se dedica su esposa?**	Ah kay say daydeekah soo ayspoasah?
My wife works at a transport agency.	**Mi mujer trabaja en una agencia de transportes.**	Mee mookhehr trahbahkhah ayn oonah ahkhanthyah day trahnspoartayss.
Where do you work?	¿**Dónde trabaja usted?**	Doanday trahbahkhah oostaydh?
I work in New York.	**Trabajo en Nueva York.**	Trahbahkhoa ayn Nwaybah Yoark.
Where does your son work?	¿**Dónde trabaja su hijo?**	Doanday trahbahkhah soo eekhoa?
He works at the local library.	**Trabaja en la biblioteca local.**	Trahbahkhah ayn lah beeblyotaykah loakahl.

Vocabulary - Vocabulario

agency	**agencia**	ahkhaynthyah
friend	**amigo**	ahmeegoa
years	**años**	ahnyoass
baby	**bebé**	baybhay
library	**biblioteca**	beeblyotaykah
carpenter	**carpintero**	kahrpeentayroa
married	**casado**	kahssahdhoa
dentist	**dentista**	daynteestah
age	**edad**	aydhahdh
businessman	**empresario**	aympraysahryo
wife	**esposa, mujer**	ayspoasah, mookhehr
to earn	**ganar**	gahnahr
daughter	**hija**	eekhah
son	**hijo**	eekhoa
children	**hijos**	eekhoass
mother	**madre**	mahdray
mechanic	**mecánico**	maykahneekoa
doctor	**médico**	mehdheekoa
months	**meses**	mayssayss
your	**suyo**	sooyoa
they work	**trabajan**	trahbahkhahn
job	**trabajo**	trahbahkhoa
transport	**transporte**	trahnspoartayss

At the travel agent's
En la agencia de viajes

Can I have a second class ticket to Glasgow, please?	¿Me da un billete de segunda a Glasgow, por favor?	May dah oon beelyay-tay day saygoondah ah Glahshgow, porr fahbhor?
I want two second class returns to New York, please.	Quiero dos billetes de ida y vuelta, segunda clase, a Nueva York, por favor.	Kyayroa doss beelyay-tayss day eedhah ee bwehltah, saygoondah klahssay, ah Nwaybah Yoark, porr fahbhor.
I'm going to Bilbao. Can I have a sleeper for tonight?	Voy a Bilbao. ¿Me da una litera para esta noche?	Boay ah Beelbahoa. May dah oonah leetayrah pahrah aystah noachay?
Can I have a first class single to Mexico?	¿Me da un billete de primera a Mexico?	May dah oon beelyay-tay day preemayrah ah Mexico?
I want a plane ticket to Buenos Aires, please.	Quiero un billete de avión a Buenos Aires, por favor.	Kyayroa oan beelyaytay day ahbhyon ah Booaynoass ighrays, porr fahbhor.
Are there any flights to Canary Islands next Wednesday?	¿Hay vuelos a Canarias el próximo miércoles?	Igh bwayloass ah Kahnahreeahs ayl prokseemoa myayrkoaleyss?
Can I have two tickets to Los Angeles?	¿Me da dos billetes para Los Angeles?	May dah doss beelyaytayss pahrah loass Ahngaylayss?
Can I have two return tickets for Sunday April 10?	¿Me da dos billetes de ida y vuelta para el domingo 10 de abril?	Mee dah doss beelyaytayss day eedhah ee bwehltah pahrah ayl doameengoa dyayth day ahbreel?
We'd like to go on a cruise, what do you have?	Quisiéramos ir en un crucero, ¿qué tienen?	Kysayrahmoass eer ayn oan kroothayroa. Kay tyaynayn?

What cruises do you have in August?	¿Qué cruceros tienen en agosto?	Kay kroothayroass tyaynayn ayn ahgoastoa?
Is there a cruise round the Caribbean Sea in June?	¿Hay algún crucero por el Caribe en junio?	Igh ahlgoon kroothayroa porr ayl kahreebay ayn khoonyoa?
What cruises do you have in May?	¿Qué cruceros tienen en mayo?	Kay kroohtayroass tyaynayn ayn mahyoa?
We are looking for a little house to hire in July.	Estamos buscando una casita para alquilar en julio.	Aystahmoass booskahndoa oonah kahseetah pahrah ahlkeelahr ayn khoolyoa.
We want to rent a car too.	También queremos alquilar un coche.	Tahmbyayn kayraymoass ahlkeelahr oon koachay.
Do you have an apartment near the sea?	¿Tiene algún apartamento en la costa?	Tyaynay ahlgoon ahpahrtahmayntoa ayn lah koastah?
Is there a camping site you can recommend?	¿Hay algún camping que me pueda recomendar?	Igh ahlgoon kahmpeeng kay may pwahdhah raykoamayndahr?
I want to go on a trek to the Himalayas.	Quiero ir a hacer treking al Himalaya.	Kyayroa eer ah ahthayr traykeen ahl eemahlahyah.
I'd like to cross the Sahara on a camel.	Me gustaría cruzar el Sahara en un camello.	May goostahryah kroothahr ayl Sahkhahrah ayn oon kahmaylyoa.
Is there an excursion over the Andes?	¿Hay alguna excursión a los Andes?	Igh ahlgoonah aykskoorsyon ah loass Ahndayss?
I'd like to ride a horse across the country.	Me gustaría cruzar el país a caballo.	May goostahryah kroothahr ayl pahees ah kahbahlyoa.
Can I have a pamphlet about Paris?	Me da un folleto sobre París?	May dah oon foalyaytoa soabray Pahrees?
Do you have any information about Morocco?	¿Tiene información acerca de Marruecos?	Tyaynay eenformahthyon ahthehrkah day mahrrooaykoass?
I'd like to have a pamphlet about Mexico.	Quisiera un folleto sobre Méjico.	Kysyayrah oon foalyaytoa soabray maykheekoa.

Can I have a guide on Acapulco's entertainment?	**Me da una guía de los entretenimientos de Acapulco.**	May dah oonah geeah day loass ayntraytayneemyayntoass day Ahkahpoolkoa.
Do you have a guide of the theatres and cinemas?	**¿Tiene usted una guía de los teatros y cines?**	Tyaynay oostaydh oonah geeah day loass tayahtroass ee theenayss?

Vocabulary - Vocabulario

August	**agosto**	ahgoastoa
to hire	**alquilar**	ahlkeelahr
apartment	**apartamento**	ahpahrtahmayntoa
plane ticket	**billete de avión**	beelyaytay day ahbhyon
guided	**con guía**	kon geeah
cruise	**crucero**	kroothayroa
excursion	**excursión**	aykskoorsyon
return	**ida y vuelta**	eedhah ee bwehltah
June	**junio**	khoonyoa
July	**julio**	khoolyoa
sleeper	**litera**	leetayhrah
can I have?	**¿me da?**	may dah?
I'd like	**me gustaría**	may goostahryah
a second class	**segunda clase**	saygoondah klahssay
next week	**la semana próxima**	lah saymahnah proakseemah
spend	**pasar**	pahsahr
round	**por**	porr
first class	**primera clase**	preemayrah klahssay
to travel	**viajar**	byahkhahr
flights	**vuelos**	bwayloass

At the bank
En el banco

I want to cash this travel(l)er's cheque/check please.	**Quiero cobrar este cheque de viaje, por favor.**	Kyayroa koabrahr aystay chaykay day byahkhay, porr fahbhor.
I'd like to change some pesetas, please.	**Quisiera cambiar unas pesetas, por favor.**	Keessyayrah kahmbyahr oonahss paysaytahss, porr fahbhor.
We'd like to get some pounds.	**Quisiéramos conseguir unas libras.**	Keessyayrahmoass konsaygeer oonahss leebrahss.
Can I have some German Marks, please?	**¿Me da unos marcos alemanes, por favor?**	May dah oonoass mahrkoass ahlaymahnayss, porr fahbhor?
I want 100 Irish pounds, please.	**Quiero cien libras irlandesas, por favor.**	Kyayroa thyayn leebrahss erlahndaysahss, porr fahbhor.
May I have some American dollars, please?	**¿Me da unos dólares americanos, por favor?**	May dah oonoass doalahrayss ahmayreekahnoass, porr fahbhor?
What's the rate of exchange?	**¿A cómo está el cambio?**	Ah koamoa aystah ayl kahmbyoa?
How much do you charge in commission?	**¿Cuánto cobran de comisión?**	Kwahntoa koabrahn day koameessyon?
How many pesos do I get for a dollar?	**¿Cuántos pesos me dan por un dolar?**	Kwahntoass payssoass may dahn porr oon doalahr?
May I cash this cheque, please?	**¿Puedo hacer efectivo este cheque, por favor?**	Pwaydhoa ahthayr ayfaykteebhoa aystay chaykay, porr fahbhor?
Can you cash a personal cheque?	**¿Puedo hacer efectivo un cheque personal?**	Pwaydhoa ahthayr ayfaykteebhoa oon chaykay pehrsoanahl?

Where can I cash these traveller's cheques?	¿Dónde puedo cobrar estos cheques de viaje?	Doanday pwaydhoa koabrahr aystoass chaykayss day byahkhay?
Will you take a personal cheque?	¿Cogerán un cheque personal?	Kokhayrahn oon chaykay pehrsoanahl?
Please credit this cheque to my account.	Quiere cargar este cheque en mi cuenta, por favor.	Kyaray kahrgahr aystay chaykay ayn mee kwayntay, porr fahbhor?
Sign here, please.	Firme aquí, por favor.	Feermay ahkee, porr fahbhor.
The cheque is crossed, it can't be cashed.	Este cheque está cruzado, no se puede hacer efectivo.	Aystay chaykay aystah kroothahdoa, noa say pwaydhay ahthayr ayfaykteebhoa.
I'd like to get some cash with my credit card.	Quisiera sacar algún dinero con mi tarjeta de crédito.	Keessyayrah sahkahr ahlgoon deenayroa kon mee tahrkhaytah day kraydeetoa.
I need some money. Do you take my credit card?	Necesito algún dinero. ¿Cogen mi tarjeta de crédito?	Naythaysseetoa ahlgoon deenayroa. Kokhayn mee tahrkhaytah day kraydeetoa?
May I open an account at your bank?	¿Puedo abrir una cuenta en su banco?	Pwaydhoa ahbreer oonah kwayntah ayn soo bahnkoa?
I'd like to open a current account.	Quisiera abrir una cuenta corriente.	Keessyayrah ahbreer oonah kwayntah koarryayntay.
Could I open a deposit account?	¿Puedo abrir una cartilla de ahorro?	Pwaydhoa ahbreer oonah kahrteelya day ahoarroa?
I want to open a bank account.	Quiero abrir una cuenta bancaria.	Kyayroa ahbreer oonah kwayntah bahnkahryah.
When can I have my chequebook/ checkbook?	¿Cuándo me darán el talonario?	Kwahndoa may dahrahn ayl tahloanahryoa?

Can I have my chequebook/ checkbook today?	**¿Me pueden dar el talonario hoy?**	May pwaydhayn dahr ayl tahloanahryoa oy?
I arranged for some money to be transferred from London. Has it arrived yet?	**Estoy esperando una transferencia de Londres. ¿No ha llegado todavía?**	Aystoy ayspayrahndoa oonah trahnsfayrayntheeah day Lohndrays. Noa ah lyaygahdhoa toadhahbheeah?
I'm expecting some money from America. Has it arrived yet?	**Estoy esperando algún dinero de América. ¿No ha llegado todavía?**	Aystoy ayspayrahndoa ahlgoon deenayroa day Amayreekah. Noa ah lyaygahdhoa toadhahbheeah?
I'd like to draw up a letter of credit.	**Quisiera abrir una carta de crédito.**	Keesyayrah ahbreer oonah kahrtah day kraydeetoa.
I'm an importer and need a letter of credit.	**Soy importador y necesito una carta de crédito.**	Soay eempoartahdoar eeh naythaysseetoa oonah kahrtah day kraydeetoa.
Can I draw up a letter of credit at this bank?	**¿Puedo abrir una carta de crédito en este banco?**	Pwaydhoa ahbreer oonah kahrtah day kraydeetoa ayn aystay bahnkoa?
Do you want my account number?	**¿Quiere el número de mi cuenta?**	Kyayray ayl noomayroa day mee kwayntah?

Vocabulary - **Vocabulario**

change	**cambiar**	kahmbyahr
rate of exchange	**el cambio**	ayl kahmbyoa
letter of credit	**carta de crédito**	kahrtah day kraydeetoa
deposit account	**cartilla de ahorros**	karteelyah day ahorroass
cheque/check	**cheque**	chaykay
travel(l)er's cheques	**cheques de viaje**	chaykayss day byahkhay

cash	**cobrar**	koabrahr
charge	**cobrar**	koabrahr
commission	**comisión**	koameessyon
credit	**crédito**	kraydeetoa
crossed	**cruzado**	kroothadoa
account	**cuenta**	kwayntah
current account	**cuenta corriente**	kwayntah koarryayntay
expect	**esperar**	ayspayrahr
exporter	**exportador**	aykspoartahdoar
draw up	**extender, abrir**	aykstayndayr, ahbreer
sign	**firmar**	feermahr
importer	**importador**	eempoartahdoar
arrive	**llegar**	lyaygahr
account number	**el número de la cuenta**	ayl noomayroa day lah kwayntah
chequebook	**talonario**	tahloanahryo
credit card	**tarjeta de crédito**	tahrkhaytah day kraydeetoa
transfer	**transferencia**	trahnsfayrayntheeah
travel(l)er	**viajero**	byahkhayroa

Buying in a department store	Comprando en unos grandes almacenes	
Where can I buy toys/records?	¿Dónde puedo comprar juguetes, discos?	Doanday pwaydhoa komprahr khoogaytays/ deeskoass?
Where can I buy a film for my camera?	¿Dónde puedo comprar un carrete para mi cámara?	Doanday pwaydhoa komprahr oon kahrraytay pahrah mee kahmahrah?
Where's the men's department?	¿Dónde está la sección de caballeros?	Doanday aystah lah saykthyon day kabahlyayroass?
Where's the music/sports department?	¿Dónde está la sección de música/ deportes?	Doanday aystah lah saykthyon day moossee- kah/daypoartayss?
The cosmetics department, please.	La sección de cosmética, por favor.	Lah saykthyon day koasmayteekah, porr fahbhor.
The restaurant floor, please.	La planta del restaurante, por favor.	Lah plahntah dayl raystowrahntay, porr fahbhor.
The toys section, please.	La sección de juguetes, por favor.	Lah saykthyon day khoo- gaytayss, porr fahbhor.
I'd like to buy a pair of trousers/ an overcoat.	Quisiera comprar un par de pantalo- nes/un abrigo.	Keessyayrah komprahr oon pahr day pahntahloa- nayss/oon ahbreegoa.
I'd like to see some pullovers, please.	Quisiera ver algu- nos jerseys, por favor.	Keessyayrah bayr ahlgoonoas kharsayss, porr fahbhor.
We'd like to see the skirts, please.	Quisiera ver las faldas, por favor.	Keesyayrah bayr lahs fahldahs, porr fahbhor.
I'd like to buy a shirt.	Me gustaría com- prar una camisa.	May goostahryah komprahr oonah kahmeesah.

I'd like some writing paper/a road map/a pocket dictionary.	**Quisiera papel de escribir/un mapa de carreteras/un diccionario de bolsillo.**	Keesyayrah pahpehl day ayskreebheer/oon mahpah day kahrraytayrahss/oon deekthyoanahryoa day boalseelyoa.
Do you have a map of Madrid/stamps/magazines?	**¿Tiene usted un mapa de Madrid/sellos/revistas?**	Tyaynay oostaydh oon mahpah day Madreedh/saylyoass/raybheestahs?
Can I have a ball pen/fountain pen/today's paper?	**¿Me da un bolígrafo /una pluma estilográfica / el periódico de hoy?**	May dah oon boalee-grahfoa / oonah ploomah aysteeloagrahfeekah/ayl payryodheekoa day oy?
How much is that dress/leather bag/skirt?	**¿Cuánto es ese vestido/bolso de cuero/falda?**	Kwahntoa ayss aysay baysteedhoa/boalsoa day kwayroa/fahldah?
How much are those shoes/gloves?	**¿Qué valen esos zapatos/guantes?**	Kay bahlayn aysoass thahpahtoass/gwahntayss?
I like this dress. I'll take it.	**Me gusta ese vestido. Me lo quedo.**	May goostah aysay baysteedhoa. May loa kaydhoa.
I like those shoes. I'll take them.	**Me gustan esos zapatos. Me los quedo.**	May goostahn aysoass thahpahtoass. May loass kaydhoa.
Can you show me that bracelet/gold chain/silver broach?	**¿Me enseña esa pulsera/cadena de oro/broche de plata?**	May aynsaynnyah aysah poolsayrah / kahdhaynah day oaroa/brochay day plahtah?
I'd like to see that watch/some rings/a wedding ring.	**Quisiera ver ese reloj/unos anillos/una alianza.**	Keesyayrah bayr aysay rehlokh/oonoass ahneelyoass/oonah ahleeahnthah.
No, not that one. The one next to it/the one behind it.	**No, ése no. El que está junto a él/El que está detrás.**	Noa, aysay noa, Ayl kay aystah khoontoa ah ayl/Ayl kay aystah daytrahss.
I want the one in front/the silver one.	**Quiero el que está delante/el de plata.**	Kyayroa ayl kay aystah daylahntay/ayl day plahtah.

I like the blue stone/the yellow one.	**Me gusta la piedra azul/la amarilla.**	May goostah lah peeayhdrah ahthool/lah ahmahreelyah.
Give me the thin bracelet/the thick one.	**Deme la pulsera delgada/la gruesa.**	Daymay lah poolsayrah daylgahdah/lah grwaysah.
Can I try on this dress/these trousers/this pullover?	**¿Puedo probarme este vestido/estos pantalones/este jersey?**	Pwaydhoa proabahrmay aystay baysteedhoa/ aystoass pahntahloanayss/aystay khayrsay?
Where can I try on this suit/this dress?	**¿Dónde puedo probarme este traje/este vestido?**	Doanday pwaydoa proabahrmay aystay trahkhay /aystay baysteedhoa?
Where's the fitting room?	**¿Dónde está el probador?**	Doanday aystah ayl proabahdhoar?
Where do I have to pay?	**¿Dónde tengo que pagar?**	Doanday tayngoa kay pahgahr?
Where's the cash desk?	**¿Dónde está la caja?**	Doanday aystah lah kahkhah?
Where's the cashier?	**¿Dónde está la cajera?**	Doanday aystah lah kahkhayrah?

Vocabulary - **Vocabulario**

overcoat	**abrigo**	ahbreegoa
wedding ring	**alianza**	ahleeahnthah
the yellow one	**la amarilla**	lah ahmahreelyah
ring	**anillo**	ahneelyoa
ball pen	**bolígrafo**	boaleegrahfoa
leather bag	**bolso de cuero**	boalsoa day kwayroa
silver broach	**broche de plata**	broachay day plahtah
gold chain	**cadena de oro**	kahdaynah day oaroa
cash desk	**caja**	kahkhah
cashier	**cajera**	kahkhayrah
camera	**cámara**	kahmahrah
shirt	**camisa**	kahmeesah
film	**carrete, película**	kahrraytay, payleekoolah
cosmetics	**cosméticos**	koasmayteekoass
thin	**delgado**	daylgahdoa

sport	**deporte**	daypoartay
pocket dictionary	**diccionario de bolsillo**	deekthyoanahryoa day boalseelyoa
records	**discos**	deeskoass
skirt	**falda**	fahldah
thick	**grueso**	grwaysoa
gloves	**guantes**	gwahntayss
pullover	**jersey**	khersay
toys	**juguetes**	khoogaytayss
road map	**mapa de carreteras**	mahpah day kahrraytayrahss
music	**música**	moosseekah
pay	**pagar**	pahgahr
trousers	**pantalones**	pahntahloanayss
writing paper	**papel de escribir**	pahpehl day ayskreebheer
pair	**par**	pahr
today's paper	**periódico de hoy**	payryodheekoa day oy
the blue stone	**la piedra azul**	lah peeaydrah ahthool
the silver one	**el de plata**	ayl day plahtah
fountain pen	**pluma estilográfica**	ploomah aysteeloagrahfeekah
fitting room	**probador**	proabahdhoar
try on	**probarse**	proabahrsay
bracelet	**pulsera**	poolsayrah
watch	**reloj**	rehlokh
magazines	**revistas**	raybheestahs
stamps	**sellos**	saylyoass
suit	**traje**	trahkhay
dress	**vestido**	baysteedhoa
shoes	**zapatos**	thahpahtoass
the one next to it	**el que está junto a él**	ayl kay aystah khoontoa ah ayl
the one behind it	**el que está detrás**	ayl kay aystah daytrahss
the one in front	**el que está delante**	ayl kay aystah daylahntay

At the doctor's
En el médico

Can you get me a doctor?	**¿Puede llamar al médico?**	Pwaydhay lyahmahr ahl mehdheekoa?
Is there a doctor here?	**¿Hay algún médico aquí?**	Igh ahlgoon mehdheekoa ahkee?
I need a doctor - quick.	**Necesito un médico -rápido.**	Naythayseetoa oon mehdheekoa, rahpeedhoa.
Where can I find a doctor?	**¿Dónde puedo encontrar un médico?**	Doanday pwaydhoa aynkontrahr oon mehdheekoa?
Where's the surgery?	**¿Dónde está la consulta?**	Doonday aystah lah koansooltah?
What are the surgery hours?	**¿Cuáles son las horas de consulta?**	Kwahlayss son lahss oarahss day koansooltah?
Could the doctor come to see me?	**¿Podría venir el médico a verme?**	Poadreeah bayneer ayl mehdheekoa ah bayrmay?
What time can the doctor come?	**¿A qué hora puede venir el médico?**	Ah kay oarah pwaydhay bayneer ayl mehdeekoa?
Can I have an appointment?	**¿Me puede dar hora?**	May pwaydhay dahr oarah?
Good morning, doctor. I don't feel well.	**Buenos días, doctor. No me encuentro bien.**	Bwaynoass deeahss, doaktoar. Noa may aynkwayntroa byayn.
I've got a terrible headache.	**Tengo un dolor de cabeza terrible.**	Tayngoa oon doalor day kahbhaythah tayrreeblay.
I have a pain here.	**Tengo un dolor aquí./ (Me duele aquí).**	Tayngoa oon doalor ahkee. May dwaylay ahkee.
I have a pain in my chest.	**Tengo un dolor en el pecho./ (Me duele el pecho).**	Tayngoa oon doalor ayn ayl paychoa. May dwaylay ayl paychoa.

I've got a stomach-ache.	**Tengo dolor de estómago.**	Tayngoa doalor day aystomahgoa.
I've been vomiting and I feel sick.	**He estado vomitando y estoy mareado.**	Ay aystahdoa boameetahndoa ee aystoy mahrayahdhoa.
I have a cold	**Tengo catarro.**	Tayngoa kahtahrroa.
I'm constipated.	**Estoy estreñido.**	Aystoy aystrehnyeedhoa.
I've got diarrhoea.	**Tengo diarrea.**	Tayngoa dyahrrayah.
Do you have fever/a temperature?	**¿Tiene usted fiebre?**	Tyaynay oostaydh fyehbray?
Do you have a pain?	**¿Tiene usted algún dolor?**	Tyaynay oostaydh ahlgoon doalor?
Have you had this pain before?	**¿Ha tenido este dolor antes?**	Ah tayneedoa aystay doalor ahntays?
Have you ever had a heart attack?	**¿Ha tenido algún infarto alguna vez?**	Ah tayneedoa ahlgoon eenfahrtoa ahlgoonah bayth?
Do you have difficulties breathing?	**¿Tiene dificultades al respirar?**	Tyaynay deefeekooltahdhayss ahl rayspeerahr?
Have you been vaccinated against tetanus?	**¿Está vacunado contra el tétano?**	Aystah bahkoonahdoa kontrah ayl taytahnoa?
Where does it hurt?	**¿Dónde le duele?**	Doanday lay dwaylay?
What kind of pain is it?	**¿Qué clase de dolor es?**	Kay klassay day doalor ayss?
Is it a dull or sharp pain?	**¿Es un dolor apagado o agudo?**	Ays oon doalor ahpahgahdoa oa ahgoodhoa?
Is it a throbbing or constant pain?	**¿Es un dolor palpitante o constante?**	Ays oon doalor pahlpeetahntay oa konstahntay?
Doctor, I have period pains.	**Doctor, tengo dolores menstruales.**	Doaktoar, tayngoa doaloarays maynstrooahlyss.
I have a vaginal infection	**Tengo una infección vaginal.**	Taungoa oonah eenfaykthyon bahkheenahl.
I'm on the pill	**Tomo la píldora.**	Toamoa lah peeldoarah.

haven't had my period for three months.	**Llevo tres meses sin menstruación.**	Lyayboa trayss mayssayss seen maynstrooahthyon.
Doctor, I'm pregnant.	**Doctor, estoy embarazada.**	Doaktoar, aystoy aymbahrahthahdhah.
have a pain in my left breast.	**Tengo un dolor en el pecho izquierdo.**	Tayngoa oon doalor ayn ayl paychoa eethkyayrdoa.
How long have you been feeling like this?	**¿Cuánto tiempo lleva sintiéndose así?**	Kwahntoa tyaympoa lyaybah seentyayndoasay ahsee?
s it the first time you've had this?	**¿Es la primera vez que tiene esto?**	Ayss lah preemayrah bayth kay tyaynay aystoa?
Undress down to the waist.	**Desnúdese hasta la cintura.**	Daysnoodaysay ahstah lah theentoorah.
Lie down over there.	**Túmbese ahí.**	Toombaysay ahee.
Breathe deeply.	**Respire profundamente.**	Rayspeeray proafoondahmayntay.
Does it hurt here?	**¿Le duele aquí?**	Lay dwaylay ahkee?
want a specimen of your blood/urine.	**Quiero una muestra de su sangre/orina.**	Kyayroa oonah mwaystrah day soo sahngray/oareenah?
want you to go to the hospital for a general check-up.	**Quiero que vaya usted al hospital para un chequeo.**	Kyayroa kay bahyah oostaydh ahl oaspeetahl pahrah oon chaykayoa.
You'll have to have an operation.	**Tendrá que operarse.**	Tayndrah kay oapayrahrsay.
want you to see a specialist.	**Quiero que vaya a ver a un especialista.**	Kyayroa kay bahyah ah bayr ah oon ayspaytheeahleestah.
You must stay in bed for three days.	**Debe de quedarse tres días en cama.**	Daybay day kaydahrsay trayss deeahss ayn kahmah.
You have a vaginal infection.	**Tiene una infección vaginal.**	Tyaynay oonah eenfaykthyon bahkheenahl.
Take this prescription to the chemist.	**Lleve esta receta a una farmacia.**	Lyaybay aystah raythaytah ah oonah fahrmahthyah.

Take these pills three times a day.	**Tome estas pastillas tres veces al día.**	Toamay aystahss pahsteelyahss trayss baythayss ahl deeah.
I'll give you an injection.	**Le daré una inyección.**	Lay dahray oonah eenyaykthyon.
I'll put you on a diet.	**Le pondré a dieta.**	Lay poandray ah deeaytah.
Come to see me in two days.	**Venga a verme dentro de dos días.**	Vayngah ah bayrmay dayntroa day doss deeahss.
You must be X-rayed.	**Debe de hacerse una placa de rayos X.**	Daybay day ahthayrsay oonah plahkah day rahyoass aykees.
Stay in bed for a few days.	**Quédese unos días en cama.**	Kaydaysay oonoass deeahs ayn kahmah.
Can you give me a prescription for this?	**¿Me puede dar una receta para esto?**	May pwaydhay dahr oonah raythaytah pahrah aystoa?
Can you prescribe me some sleeping pills?	**¿Me puede recetar unas píldoras para dormir?**	May pwaydhay raythaytahr oonahss peeldorahss pahrah doarmeer?
This is the usual medicine.	**Esta es la medicina normal.**	Aystah ayss lah maydheetheenah noarmahl.
I'm allergic to antibiotics.	**Soy alérgico a los antibióticos.**	Soy ahlehrkheekoa ah loass ahnteebhyoateekoass.
I don't want anything too strong.	**No quiero nada demasiado fuerte.**	Noa kyayroa nahdah daymahssyahdhoa fwayrtay.
How many times a day should I take it?	**¿Cuántas veces al día debería tomarla?**	Kwahntahs baythayss ahl deeah daybayreeah toamahrlah?
What treatment are you having?	**¿Qué tratamiento sigue usted?**	Kay trahtahmyayntoa seegay oostaydh?
What medicine are you taking?	**¿Qué medicinas está tomando?**	Kay maydheetheenahss aystah toamahndoa?
What's your normal dose?	**¿Cuál es la dosis normal?**	Kwahl ayss lah doassees noarmahl?

Injection or oral?	¿Inyección o vía oral?	Eenyaykthyon oa beeah oarahl?
Are you allergic to antibiotics?	¿Es usted alérgico a los antibióticos?	Ayss oostaydh ahlehrkheekoa ah loas ahnteebhyoateekoass?
Have you been operated on for appendicitis?	¿Le han operado de apendicitis?	Lay ahn oapayrahdoa day ahpayndeethee- tees?
Have you had a venereal disease?	¿Ha tenido usted alguna enfermedad venérea?	Ah tayneedoa oostaydh ahlgoonah aynfayrmaydahdh baynayrayah?
How much do I owe you, doctor?	¿Cuánto le debo, doctor?	Kwahntoa lay daybhoa, doaktoar?
May I have a receipt for my Health Insurance?	¿Me puede dar un recibo para mi Seguro de Enfermedad?	May pwaydhay dahr oon raytheeboa pahrah mee saygooroa day aynfayrmaydahdh?
Can I have a medical certifi- cate?	¿Me da un certifica- do médico?	May dah oon thayrteefeekahdhoa maydheekoa?
Would you fill in this health insur- ance form, please?	¿Le importaría rellenar este impre- so del seguro de enfermedad?	Lay eempoartahreeah raylyaynahr aystay eemprayssoa dayl saygooroa day aynfayrmaydahdh?
What are the visiting hours?	¿Cuáles son las horas de visita?	Kwahlayss son lahss oorahss day beeseetah?
Can I get up?	¿Puedo levantar- me?	Pwaydhoa laybhantahrmay?
When will the doc- tor come?	¿Cuándo vendrá el médico?	Kwahndoa bayndrah ayl maydheekoa?
I'm in pain.	Tengo un dolor./ (Me duele).	Tayngoa oon doalor/ May dwaylay.
Can I have a pain killer?	¿Me da un calmante?	May dah oon kahlmahntay?
Do I need a blood transfusion?	¿Necesito una trans- fusión de sangre?	Naythayseetoa oona trahnsfoosyon day sahngray.

Vocabulary - **Vocabulario**

sharp	**agudo**	ahgoodhoa
allergic	**alérgico**	ahlehrkheekoa
dull	**apagado**	ahpahgahdhoa
constant	**constante**	konstahntay
surgery	**consulta**	konsooltah
diarrohea	**diarrea**	dyahrrayah
diet	**dieta**	deeaytah
difficulty	**dificultad**	deefeekooltahdh
pain	**dolor**	doalor
headache	**dolor de cabeza**	doalor day kahbhaythah
stomachache	**dolor de estómago**	doalor day aystoamahgoa
period pains	**dolores menstruales**	doaloarayss maynstrooahlayss
to sleep	**dormir**	doarmeer
hurts	**duele**	dwaylay
to find	**encontrar**	aynkontrahr
constipated	**estreñido**	aystrehnyeedhoa
chemist's	**farmacia**	fahrmahthyah
fever	**fiebre**	feeayhbray
appointment	**hora**	oarah
heart attack	**infarto**	eenfahrtoa
infection	**infección**	eenfaykthyon
injection	**inyección**	eenyaykthyon
ointment	**linimento**	leeneemayntoa
sick/dizzy	**mareado**	mahrayahdhoa
medicine	**medicina**	maydeetheenah
doctor	**médico**	mehdheekoa
I need	**necesito**	naythayseetoa
ointment	**linimento**	leeneemayntoa
palpitating	**palpitante**	pahlpeetahntay
chest	**pecho (hombre)**	paychoa

breast	**pecho (mujer)**	paychoa
pills	**píldoras**	peeldoarahs
prescription	**receta**	raythaytah
to prescribe	**recetar**	raythaytahr
breathing	**respiración**	rayspeerahthyon
to feel	**sentir**	saynteer
tetanus	**tétano**	taytahnoa
vaccinated	**vacunado**	bahkoonahdhoa
vaginal	**vaginal**	bahkheenahl
vomiting	**vomitando**	boameetahndhoa
antibiotics	**antibióticos**	ahnteebhyoateekoass
apendicitis	**apendicitis**	ahpayndeetheetees
aspirins	**aspirinas**	ahspeereenahss
pain-killing	**calmante**	kahlmahntay
sweets	**caramelos**	kahrahmayloass
cold	**catarro**	kahtahrroah
check up	**chequeo**	chaykayoa
waist	**cintura**	theentoorah
undress	**desnúdese**	daysnoodaysay
diarrhoea	**diarrea**	dyahrrayah
dosis	**dosis**	doasees
pregnant	**embarazada**	aymbahrahthahdhah
illness	**enfermedad**	aynfayrmaydahdh
specialist	**especialista**	ayspaytheeahleestah
visiting hours	**horas de visita**	oarahss day beeseetah
get up	**levantarme**	laybahntahrmay
sample	**muestra**	mwaystrah
to have an operation	**operarse**	oapayrahrsay
urine	**orina**	oareenah
toothpaste	**pasta de dientes**	pahstah day dyayntayss

deeply	**profundamente**	proafoondahmayntay
to stay	**quedarse**	kaydahrsay
breathe	**respirar**	rayspeerahr
mint-flavour	**sabor a menta**	sahboar ah mayntah
blood	**sangre**	sahngray
health insurance	**seguro de enfermedad**	saygooroa day aynfayrmaydahdh
transfusion	**transfusión**	trahnsfoosyon
lie down	**túmbese**	toombaysay
vagina	**vagina**	bahkheenah
venereal	**venérea**	baynayrayah

Chemist's /
drugstore
Farmacia

Can I have some aspirins, please?	**¿Me da unas aspirinas, por favor?**	May dah oonahs ahspeereeahs porr fahborr?
Give me some sleeping pills, please.	**Déme unos somníferos, por favor.**	Denmay oonahs somneeferrohs porr fahborr.
Can I have some sweets/candies for the throat?	**¿Me da unos caramelos de menta para la garganta?**	May dah oonahs kahrahmaylohs day mayntah pahrah lah gargahntah?
Give me something for diarrhoea.	**Déme algo para la diarrea.**	Demmay algoh pahrah lah deehrayah.
I'd like to have something for my cough.	**Me gustaría tomar algo para la tos.**	May goostahreeah toamarr algoh pahrah lah toss.
Toothpaste, please.	**Pasta de dientes, por favor.**	Pahstah day deeyentays porr fahborr.
Can I have some liniment?	**¿Me da linimento?**	May dah leeneementoh?
Where is there a chemist's?	**¿Dónde hay una farmacia?**	Doanday I oohan farmathyah?
Can you prepare this prescription?	**¿Puede Ud. preparar esta receta?**	Pwayday oostayth prepahrarr aystah raythaytah?
Can I get it without prescription?	**¿Puedo obtenerlo sin receta?**	Pwaydoh obtaynerloa sin raythaytah?

Vocabulary - **Vocabulario**

cold	**catarro**	kahtahrroa
hay fever	**fiebre del heno**	fyebray
sickness	**mareo**	marayoh
indigestion	**indisgestión**	eendeehessteeohn
sun burnt	**quemaduras de sol**	kaymahdoorahs day sol
cough	**tos**	toss
cotton	**algodón**	ahlgoadonn
aspirins	**aspirinas**	ahspeereenahs
contraceptives	**anticonceptivos**	antikontheypteeboass
desifectants	**desinfectantes**	daysinfayctahntays
digestive	**digestivo**	deehesteeboa
sticking plaster	**esparadrapo**	ayspahrahdrahpoa
gargles	**gárgaras**	gahrgahrahs
gauze	**gasa**	gashah
ear-drops	**gotas para los oídos**	gohtahs pahrah lohs oheedohs
eye-drops	**gotas para los ojos**	gohtahs pahrah lohs ohohs
laxative	**laxante**	lahxantay
sanitary towel	**compresas**	coampraysahss
cough tablets	**pastillas para la tos**	pahstilyahs pahrah lah toss
sedative	**sedante**	saydahntay
slipping pills	**somniferos**	somneeferrohs
calcium tablets	**tabletas de calcio**	tahblaytahs day kahltheeoa
tampons	**tampones**	tahmpohnays
plaster	**tiritas**	teereetahs
horns	**callos**	kahlyohs
bandage	**venda**	bayndah
sun oil	**aceite solar**	ahthaytay sohlarr
cologne	**agua de colonia**	ahgwah day kohlohneeah
toothbrush	**cepillo de dientes**	thaypeelyoh day deeayntays

shaving brush	**brocha de afeitar**	brohchah day ahfaytarr
shaving cream	**crema de afeitar**	kraymah day ahfaytarr
moisturizing cream	**crema hidratante**	kraymah eedrahtahntay
cleansing cream	**crema limpiadora**	kraymah leempeeahdohrah
hand cream	**crema para las manos**	kraymah pahrah lahs mahnohs
night cream	**crema de noche**	kraymah day nochay
shampoo	**champú**	champoo
deodorant	**desodorante**	daysohdorahntay
nail varnish	**esmalte de uñas**	aysmahltay day oonyahs
sponge	**esponja**	ayspohnha
safety pins	**imperdibles**	eemperdeeblays
soap	**jabón**	khahbohn
shaving soap	**jabón de afeitar**	khahbohn day ahfaytarr
lipstick	**lápiz de labios**	lahpeeth day lahbeeohs
eyebrow pencil	**lápiz para los ojos**	lahpeeth pahrah lohs ohohs
nail file	**lima de uñas**	leemah day oonyahs
aftershave lotion	**loción de afeitado**	lahthyohn day ahfaytahdoh
make up	**maquillaje**	mahkheelyakhee
tissues	**pañuelos de papel**	pahnywayloass day pahpayl
toilet paper	**papel higiénico**	pahpayl eekhyayneekoa
toothpaste	**pasta de dientes**	pahstah day deeayntays
perfume	**perfume**	perfoomay
tweezers	**pinzas**	peenthahs
talcum powder	**polvos de talco**	pahlbohs day tahlkoh
brilliantine	**brillantina**	brylyanteenah
comb	**peine**	paynay
hairpin/hair clip	**horquillas**	orkilyahs
fixative	**fijador**	feehadorr
rollers	**rulos**	roolohs
dye	**tinte**	teentay
lacquer/hair spray	**laca**	lahkak

Buying in a shop
or street market
**Comprando en un
mercado callejero**

Can I have a loaf of bread?	¿Me da una barra de pan?	May dah oonah bahrrah day pahn?
Give me a sack of potatoes.	Deme una bolsa de patatas.	Daymay oonah boalsah day pahtahtahss.
Can I have a pound of sugar and a packet of salt?	¿Me da una libra de azúcar y un paquete de sal?	May dah oonah leebrah day ahthookahr ee oon pahkaytay day sahl?
Give me a bottle of oil and a can of peas.	Deme una botella de aceite y un bote de guisantes.	Daymay oonah boataylyah day ahthaytay ee oon boatay day geessahntayss.
A frozen chicken, please.	Un pollo congelado, por favor.	Oon poalyoa konkhaylahdhoa, porr fahbhor.
I'd like to see some antiques, please.	Quisiera ver algunas antigüedades, por favor.	Keessyayrah bayr ahlgoonahss ahnteegwaydhahdhayss, porr fahbhor.
May I see some old pictures.	¿Me enseña algunos cuadros antiguos?	May aynsaynyah ahlgoonoass kwahdroass ahnteegwoass?
Have you got any antiques made of brass?	¿Tiene alguna antigüedad de latón?	Tyaynay ahlgoonah ahnteegwaydhahdh day lahtoan?
I'd like to see some candelabra.	Quisiera ver algunos candelabros.	Keessyayrah bayr ahlgoonoass kahndaylahbroass?
Do you have any old furniture?	¿Tienen muebles antiguos?	Tyaynayn mwayblayss ahnteegwoass?
Have you got any Louis XIV chairs?	¿Tiene sillas Luis XIV?	Tyaynayn seelyahss Looees kahtorthay?

I'd like an old Persian carpet.	**Quisiera una antigua alfombra persa.**	Keesyayrah oonah ahnteegwah ahlfoambrah payrsah.
I'd like to develop a film.	**Quisiera revelar un carrete.**	Keesyayrah raybaylahr oon kahrraytay.
Can I have this film developed by tomorrow?	**¿Me puede revelar este carrete para mañana?**	May pwaydhay raybaylahr aystay kahrraytay pahrah mahnyahnah?
When can I have this film developed?	**¿Cuándo me puede revelar este carrete?**	Kwahndhoa may pwaydhay rahbahlahr aystay kahrraytay?
Can you develop this film?	**¿Puede revelar este carrete?**	Pwaydhay raybaylahr aystay kahrraytah?
Can I have another film?	**¿Me da otro carrete?**	May dah oatroa kahrraytah?
Give me another film, please.	**Deme otro carrete, por favor.**	Daymay oatroa kahrraytay, porr fahbhor.
The price is too high for me. I can offer you 10.000 pesetas.	**El precio es demasiado alto para mí. Puedo ofrecerle 10.000 pesetas.**	Ayl praytheeoa ays daymahssyadhoa ahltoa pahrah mee. Pwaydhoa oafraythayrlay deeayth meel paysaytahs.
It's too much for me, I'm afraid.	**Me temo que es demasiado para mí.**	May taymoa kay ayss daymahssyahdhoa pahrah mee.
It's far too much. I'll give you 1.000 pts.	**Es demasiado. Le daré 1.000 pesetas.**	Ayss daymahssyahdhoa. Lay dahray meel paysaytahs.
I'll buy it for 2.000 pesetas.	**Se lo compro por 2.000 pesetas.**	Say loa koamproa porr doass meel paysaytahs.
I can't pay that much. What about 5.000 pesetas?	**No puedo pagar tanto. ¿Qué tal 5.000 pesetas?**	Noa pwaydhoa pahgahr tahntoa. Kay tahl theenkoa meel paysaytahs?
This is my last price.	**Este es mi último precio.**	Aysstay ayss mee oolteemoa praythyoa.
Not a penny more.	**Ni un peso más.**	Nee oon paysoa mahss.
Let's meet half way.	**Encontrémonos a mitad de camino.**	Aynkontraymoanoass ah meetahdh day kahmeenoa.
This is a real bargain.	**Esto es una verdadera ganga.**	Aystoa ayss oonah bayrdahdayrah gahngah.
That is a giveaway price.	**Esto es un precio regalado.**	Aystoa ayss oon praythyoa raygahlahdoa.

I'm losing money.	**Estoy perdiendo dinero.**	Aystoy payrdeeayndoa deenayroa.

Vocabulary - **Vocabulario**

oil	**aceite**	athaytay
carpet	**alfombra**	ahlfoambrah
antiques	**antigüedades**	ahnteegwaydhahdhayss
loaf	**barra (de pan)**	bahrrah (day pahn)
can	**bote**	boatay
bottle	**botella**	boataylyah
candelabra	**candelabros**	kahndaylahbroass
bargain	**chollo**	choalyoa
frozen	**congelado**	konkhaylahdoa
pictures	**cuadros**	kwahdroass
too much	**demasiado**	daymahssyahdhoa
too high	**demasiado alto**	daymahssyahdhoa ahltoa
let's meet	**encontrémonos**	aynkontraymoanoass
peas	**guisantes**	geessahntayss
brass	**latón**	lahtoan
pound	**libra**	leebrah
I'm afraid.	**me temo**	may taymoa
furniture	**muebles**	mwayblayss
offer	**oferta**	oafayrtah
packet	**paquete**	pahkaytay
film	**película, carrete**	payleekoolah, kahrraytay
losing	**perdiendo**	payrdeeayndoa
chicken	**pollo**	poalyoa
what about?	**¿qué hay de?**	kay igh day?
giveaway	**regalo**	raygahloa
develop	**revelar**	raybaylahr
sack	**saco (bolsa)**	sahkoa (boalsah)
last price	**último precio**	oolteemoa praytheeoa

On the beach
En la playa

Is there a quiet beach near here?	**¿Hay por aquí alguna playa tranquila?**	¿Igh porr ahkee ahlgoonah plahyah trankeela?
Which is the best beach?	**¿Cuál es la mejor playa?**	¿Kwahl ayss lah mekhor plahyah?
Is it safe for swimming?	**¿Es seguro para nadar aquí?**	¿Ayss sehgooroa pahrah nadahr ahkee?
Is it far to walk?	**¿Se puede ir andando?**	¿Se pwede eer ahndahndoa?
Is there a bus to the beach?	**¿Hay autobús a la playa?**	¿Igh owtohboos ah lah plahyah?
Is it safe for small children?	**¿Es seguro para niños pequeños?**	¿Ayss sehgooroa pahrah neenyoass paykaynyoass?
Are there any dangerous currents?	**¿Hay alguna corriente peligrosa?**	¿Igh algoonah korryeyntay payhleegroassah?
There's a strong current here	**Aquí hay mucha corriente.**	Ahkee igh moochah korryayntay.
Is there a lifeguard?	**¿Hay algún vigilante?**	¿Igh ahlgoon beekheelahntay?
Does it get very rough?	**¿Se pone el mar bravo?**	¿Say pohnay ayl mahr brahvoa?
What's the temperature of the water?	**¿Cuál es la temperatura del agua?**	¿Kwahl ayss lah taympayrahtoorah dayl ahgwah?
What time is high/low tide?	**¿A qué hora es la marea alta/baja?**	¿Ah kay oarah ayss lah mahrehah ahltah/bahkhah?
Is the water cold?	**¿Está fría el agua?**	¿Aysstah freeah ayl ahgwah?
It's warm	**Está caliente.**	Aysstah kahlyayntay.

Are there showers?	¿Hay duchas?	¿Igh doochahss?
Is the tide rising / falling?	¿Está la marea subiendo/bajando?	¿Aysstah lah mahrayah soobeehendoa/ bahkhandoa?
I want to hire a/an /some ... - air mattress - bathing hut - skin-diving - deck-chair - sunshade (umbrella) - surfboard - water-skis	¿Quiero alquilar ... - un colchón neumático - una cabina - un equipo de submarinismo - una tumbona - una sombrilla - una plancha de surf - unos esquíes acuáticos	Kyayroa ahlkeelahr ... - oon koalchon nayoomahteekoa - oonah kahbheenah - oon aykeepoa day soobmahreeneesmoa - oonah toomboanah - oonah soambreelyah - oonah plahnchah day surf - oonoass ayskeeayss ahkwahteekoass
Are you a strong swimmer?	¿Nada usted bien?	¿Nahdah oosstehd byayn?
What's the charge per hour?	¿Cuánto cobran por hora?	¿Kwahntoa koabrahn porr oarah?
Is it deep?	¿Hay mucha profundidad?	¿Igh moochah proafoondeedadh?
You will be out of your depth.	No se hace pie.	Noa say athay pyay.
It's dangerous	Es peligroso.	Ayss payleehgroasoa.
Where can I rent a ...? - canoe - motorboat - rowing-boat - sailing-boat	¿Dónde puedo alquilar ..? - una canoa - una motora - una barca - un velero	¿Doanday pwaydhoa ahlkeelahr ...? - oonah kahnoaah - oonah moatoarah - oonah bahrkah - oon baylehroa

Vocabulary - **Vocabulario**

beach	playa	plahyah
quiet	tranquila	trankeelah
to swim	nadar	nahdahr
safe	seguro	sehgooroa
to walk	andar	ahndahr
dangerous	peligroso	payleegroasoa

currents	**corrientes**	korryeyntayss
lifeguard	**vigilante**	beekheelahntay
rough sea	**mar picada**	mahr peekahdah
high tide	**marea alta**	mahrayah ahltah
low tide	**marea baja**	mahrayah bahkhah
warm	**caliente**	kahlyayntay
cold	**frío**	freehoa
showers	**duchas**	doochahss
to rise	**subir**	soobeehr
rising tide	**subiendo la marea**	soobeehayndoa lah mahrayah
to fall	**caer**	kahayr
falling tide	**bajando la marea**	bahkhandoa lah mahrayah
to hire	**alquilar**	ahlkeelahr
air mattress	**colchón neumático**	koalchoan nayoomahteekoa
bathing hut	**cabina**	kahbheenah
skin-diving	**equipo de submarinismo**	aykeepoa day soobmahreeneesmoa
deck-chair	**tumbona**	toomboanah
sunshade	**sombrilla**	soambreelyah
surfboard	**plancha de surf**	plahnchah day soorf
water-skis	**esquíes acuáticos**	ayskeeayss ahkwahteekoass
swimmer	**nadador**	nahdahdoar
strong swimmer	**buen nadador**	booayn nahdahdoar
deep	**profundidad**	proafoondeedadh
to charge	**cobrar**	koabrahr
depth	**profundo**	proafoondoa
rent	**alquilar**	ahlkeelahr
motorboat	**motora**	moatoarah
canoe	**canoa**	kahnoaah
rowing-boat	**barca**	bahrkah
sailing-boat	**velero**	baylehroa

At dinner and
an invitation to
dinner
**En la cena y una
invitación para cenar**

How nice of you to come!	**Han sido muy amables en venir.**	Ahn seedoa mwee ahmah-blayss ayn bayneer.
How nice to see you again!	**¡Cuánto me alegro de verles otra vez!**	Kwahntoa may ahlaygroa day bayrlayss oatrah bayth!
Welcome to our house, come in!	**Bienvenidos a nuestra casa. Pasen.**	Beeaynbayneedoass ah nwaystrah kahsah. Pahssayn.
It's nice to have you here!	**¡Cuánto me alegro de tenerles aquí!**	Kwahntoa may ahlaygroa day taynayrlayss ahkee!
It's wonderful to be here!	**¡Es maravilloso estar aquí!**	Ayss mahrahbeelyoa-ssoah aystahr ahkee!
It was very nice of you to invite us!	**Han sido ustedes muy amables en invitarnos.**	Ahn seedoa oostaydayss mwee ahmahblayss ayn eenbeetahrnoass.
I appreciate your invitation.	**Agradezco su invitación.**	Ahgrahdaythkoa soo eenbeetahthyon.
We thank you for your kind invita-tion.	**Les agradecemos su amable invitación.**	Layss ahgrahdaythhay-moass soo ahmahblay eenbeetahthyon.
You have a very nice house.	**Tienen ustedes una casa muy bonita.**	Tyaynayn oostaydayss oonah kahsah mwee boaneetah.
It's a wonderful place you have here.	**Tienen ustedes un sitio maravilloso.**	Tyaynayn oostaydayss oon seeteeoa mahrahbeelyoassoa.
It's a very pleas-ant house you have.	**Tienen ustedes una casa muy agradable**	Tyaynayn oostaydayss oonah kahsah mwee ahgrahdahblay.
Please, take a seat.	**Tomen asiento, por favor.**	Toamayn ahseeaayntoa, porr fahbhor.
You'll be comfort-able in those armchairs.	**Estarán cómodos en esos sillones.**	Aystahrahn koamoadoass ayn ayssoass seelyoahnayss.

Let me have your coats.	**Denme los abrigos.**	Daynmay loass ahbreegoass.
May I offer you something to drink.	**Me gustaría ofrecerles algo para tomar.**	May goostahreeah oafraythayrlayss ahlgoa pahrah toamahr.
Would you like to have a drink?	**¿Quieren tomar algo?**	Kyayrayn toamahr ahlgoa?
Would you like a glass of wine?	**¿Quieren tomar un vaso de vino?**	Kayrayn toamahr oon bahssoa day beenoa?
To your health.	**A su salud.**	Ah soo sahloodh.
I toast the success of our association.	**Brindo por el éxito de nuestra asociación.**	Breendoa porr ayl aykseetoa day nwaystrah ahsoatheeahthyon.
Let's make a toast.	**Brindemos.**	Breendaymoass.
Let's drink to our company's success.	**Bebamos por el éxito de nuestra compañía.**	Baybahmoass porr ayl aykseetoa day nwaystrah kompahnyeeah.
I'm drinking to your success.	**Bebo por su éxito.**	Bayboa porr soo aykseetoa.
Would you like another apperitif?	**¿Le gustaría tomar otro aperitivo?**	Lay goostahreeah toamahr oatroa ahpayreeteeboa?
Do you prefer a champagne cocktail?	**¿Prefiere usted un cóctel de champagne?**	Prayfeeayray oostaydh oon koktayl day chahmpahn?
Do you want a beer, or do you prefer cider?	**¿Quiere una cerveza o prefiere sidra?**	Kyayray oona thayrbhaythah oa prayfeeayrey seedrah?
What would you like, brandy, coñac, whisky, or perhaps a liqueur?	**¿Qué le gustaría, coñac, whisky, o quizá algún licor?**	Kay lay goostahreeah, koanyahk, weeskee, oa keethah ahlgoon leekoar?
Will you have some coffee?	**¿Quiere algo de café?**	Kyayray ahlgoa day kahfay?
White coffee or black coffee?	**¿Café con leche o sólo?**	Kahfay kon laychay oa soaloa?
A glass of orange juice, or do you prefer something stronger?	**¿Un vaso de zumo de naranja, o prefiere algo más fuerte?**	Oon bahssoa day thoomoa day nahrahnkhah, oa prayfeeayray ahlgoa mahss fwayrtay?
May I have the sauce/salt/vinegar, please?	**¿Me da la salsa/sal/vinagre, por favor?**	May dah lah sahlsah/sahl/beenahgray, porr fahbhor.

Pass me the water/sugar/bread, please.	**Páseme el agua/ el azúcar/el pan, por favor.**	Pahsaymay ayl ahgwah, ayl athookahr, ayl pahn, porr fahbhor.
May I pass you the asparagus / pepper / mayonnaise?	**¿Quiere que le pase los espárragos/la pimienta/ la mayonesa?**	Kyayray kay lay pahsay loass ayspahrrahgoass/ lah peemyayntah/lah mayoanayssah?
Can I have the salad /wine / coffee, please?	**¿Me da la ensalada/el vino/el café, por favor?**	May dah lah aynsahlahdhah/ayl beenoa/ayl kahfay, porr fahbhor?
Have another glass of wine.	**Tome otro vaso de vino.**	Toamay oatroa bahssoa day beenoa.
Would you like another cup of coffee?	**¿Le apetece otra taza de café?**	Lay ahpaytaythay oatrah tahthah day kahfay?

Vocabulary - Vocabulario

coats	**abrigos**	ahbreegoass
pleasant	**agradable**	ahgrahdahblay
water	**agua**	ahgwah
something	**algo**	ahlgoa
kind	**amable**	ahmahblay
aperitif	**aperitivo**	ahpayreeteeboa
appreciate	**apreciar**	ahpraytheeahr
sugar	**azúcar**	ahthookahr
let's drink	**bebamos**	baybahmoass
to drink	**beber**	baybayr
welcome	**bienvenido**	beeaynbayneedoa
a toast	**un brindis**	oon breendees
I toast	**brindo**	breendoa
coffee	**café**	kahfay
white coffee	**café con leche**	kahfay kon laychay
black coffee	**café sólo**	kahfay soaloa
dinner	**cena**	thaynah
cocktail	**cóctel**	koaktayl

meal	**comida**	koameedah
comfortable	**cómodo**	koamoadoa
brandy	**coñac**	koanyahk
enjoy	**disfrutar**	deesfrootahr
salad	**ensalada**	aynsahlahdah
asparagus	**espárragos**	ayspahrrahgoass
it's nice	**es estupendo**	ayss aystoopayndoa
success	**éxito**	aykseetoa
let's make	**hagamos**	ahgahmoass
liqueur	**licor**	leekoar
wonderful	**maravilloso**	mahrahbeelyoassoa
stronger	**más fuerte**	mahss fwayrtay
mayonnaise	**mayonesa**	mahyoanayssah
offer	**ofrecer**	oafraythayr
bread	**pan**	pahn
pepper	**pimienta**	peemyayntah
how nice of you	**qué amable de su parte**	kay ahmahblay day soo pahrtay
salt	**sal**	sahl
sauce	**salsa**	sahlsah
health	**salud**	sahloodh
cider	**sidra**	seedrah
armchairs	**sillones**	seelyoanayss
place	**sitio**	seeteeoa
take a seat	**tomen asiento**	toamayn ahseeayntoa
evening	**velada**	baylahdah
vinegar	**vinagre**	beenahgray
wine	**vino**	beenoa
juice	**zumo**	thoomoa

Saying
good-bye

Despidiéndose

Thank you for a wonderful dinner.	**Gracias por una cena tan maravillosa.**	Grahtyahss porr oonah thaynah tahn mahrahbeelyossah.
Dinner was wonderful/delicious.	**La cena ha sido maravillosa/ deliciosa.**	Lah thaynah ah seedoa mahrahbeelyoassah/ dayleetheeoassah.
I really enjoyed this evening.	**Lo he pasado muy bien esta noche.**	Loa ayh pahsahdoa mwee byayn aystah noachay.
We must thank you for such a lovely evening.	**Debemos darle las gracias por una velada tan maravillosa.**	Daybaymoass dahrlay lahss grathyahss porr oonah baylahdah tahn mahrahbeelyoassah.
It has been a wonderful evening.	**Ha sido una velada maravillosa.**	Ah seedoa oonah baylahdah mahrahbeelyoassah.
I must congratulate the cook.	**Debo felicitar al cocinero.**	Dayboa fayleetheetahr ahl koatheenayroa.
Congratulations to the cook.	**Felicitaciones a la cocinera.**	Fayleetheetahthyonayss ah lah koatheenayrah.
Thank you for the wonderful time I had in your country.	**Gracias por estos días tan maravillosos en su país.**	Grahthyahss porr aystoass deeahss tahn mahrahbeelyoassoass ayn soo pahees.
I really enjoyed my stay in your country.	**Lo he pasado muy bien en su país.**	Loa ay pahsahdoa mwee byayn ayn soo paheess.
I'll never forget my stay with you.	**Nunca olvidaré mi estancia con ustedes.**	Noonkah oalbeedayray mee aystahntheeah kon oostaydhayss.

Saying Good-bye - Despidiéndose

It's been wonderful to stay here with you all this time.	**Ha sido maravilloso estar aquí con ustedes todo este tiempo.**	Ah seedoa mahrahbeelyoassoa aystahr ahkee kon oostaydhayss toadoa aystah tyaympoa.
Thank you for your hospitality.	**Gracias por su hospitalidad.**	Grahthyahss porr soo oaspeetahleedhahdh.
I'll be leaving at five tomorrow.	**Me iré a las cinco mañana.**	May eeray ah lahss theenkoa mahnyahnah.
My plane is leaving at six.	**Mi avión sale a las seis.**	Mee ahbhyon sahlay ah lahss sayss.
We are leaving early in the morning.	**Salimos temprano por la mañana.**	Sahleemoass taymprahnoa porr lah mahnyahnah.
We should be home by lunch time.	**Deberíamos llegar a casa para la hora de comer.**	Daybayreeahmoass lyaygahr ah kahsah pahrah lah oarah day koamayr.
I'm taking the night train.	**Cojo el tren de noche.**	Koakhoa ayl trayn day noachay.
Give me a call when you get home.	**Telefonéame cuando llegues a casa.**	Taylayfoanayahmay kwahndhoa lyaygayss ah kahsah.
Don't forget to write.	**No te olvides de escribir.**	Noa tay oalbeedayss day ayskreebeer.
Send us a postcard when you get home.	**Mándanos una postal cuando llegues a casa.**	Mahndahnoass oonah poastahl kwahdhoa lyaygayss ah kahsah.
Have you got my telephone number?	**¿Tienes mi número de teléfono?**	Tyaynays mee noomayroa day taylayfoanoa?
Give my regards to your wife/parents/husband/family.	**Da recuerdos a tu mujer/padres/marido/familia.**	Dah raykwayrdoass ah too mookhehr/pahdrayss/mahreedhoa/fahmeelyah.
Give a kiss to the children.	**Da un beso a los niños.**	Dah oon bayssoa ah loass neenyoass.
It was a wonderful party.	**Ha sido una fiesta maravillosa.**	Ah seedoa oona feeaystah mahrahbeelyoassah.

I really enjoyed your party.	**Lo he pasado muy bien en la fiesta.**	Loa ay pahsahdhoa mwee beeayn ayn lah feeaystah.
The party was wonderful.	**La fiesta ha sido maravillosa.**	Lah feeaystah ah seedoa mahrahbeelyoassah.
Thank you for coming.	**Gracias por venir.**	Grahthyahss porr bayneer.
It was very nice of you to come.	**Ha sido usted muy amable en venir.**	Ah seedoa oostaydh mwee ahmahblay ayn bayneer.
I'm glad you enjoyed yourselves.	**Me alegro que se hayan divertido ustedes.**	May ahlaygroa kay say ahyahn deebayrteedhoa oostaydhayss.

Vocabulary - **Vocabulario**

kiss	**beso**	bayssoa
dinner	**cena**	thaynah
cook	**cocinera**	koatheenayrah
lunch	**comida**	koameedah
delicious	**deliciosa**	dayleetheeoassah
enjoy	**disfrutar**	deesfrootahr
lovely	**estupenda**	aystoopayndah
congratulate	**felicitar**	fayleetheetahr
hospitality	**hospitalidad**	oaspeetahleedhahdh
call	**llamada**	lyahmahdhah
wonderful	**maravillosa**	mahrahbeelyoassah
forget	**olvidar**	oalbeedhahr
country	**país**	paheess
for coming	**por venir**	porr bayneer
stay	**quedarse**	kaydharsay
regards	**recuerdos**	raykwayrdhoass
leaving	**saliendo**	sahleeayndhoa
early	**temprano**	taymprahnoa
night train	**tren de noche**	trayn day noachay

Countries - Países

Africa	**África**	Ahfreekah
Asia	**Asia**	Ahssyah
Australia	**Australia**	Owstrahlyah
Europe	**Europa**	Ayooroapah
North/South/Central America	**América del Norte / de Sur/Central**	Ahmayreekah dayl noartay / dayl soor/ thayntrahl
Algeria	**Argelia**	Ahrkhaylyah
Austria	**Austria**	Owstryah
Belgium	**Bélgica**	Baylkheekah
Canada	**Canadá**	Kahnahdhah
China	**China**	Cheenah
Denmark	**Dinamarca**	Deenahmahrka
England	**Inglaterra**	Eenglahtayrrah
Finland	**Finlandia**	Feenlahndyah
France	**Francia**	Frahnthyah
Germany	**Alemania**	Ahlaymahnyah
Gibraltar	**Gibraltar**	Kheebrahltahr
Great Britain	**Gran Bretaña**	Grahn braytahñah
Greece	**Grecia**	Graythyah
India	**India**	Eendyah

Ireland	**Irlanda**	Eerlahndah
Israel	**Israel**	Eesrahayl
Italy	**Italia**	Eetahlyah
Japan	**Japón**	Khahpon
Luxembourg	**Luxemburgo**	Looksaymboorgoa
Morocco	**Marruecos**	Mahrrwaykoass
Netherlands	**Países Bajos**	Paheessayss bahkhoass
New Zealand	**Nueva Zelanda**	Nwaybhah thaylahndah
Norway	**Noruega**	Noarwaygah
Portugal	**Portugal**	Portoogahl
Scotland	**Escocia**	Ayskoathyah
South Africa	**África del Sur**	Ahfreekah dayl soor
Spain	**España**	Ayspahnyah
Sweden	**Suecia**	Swaythyah
Switzerland	**Suiza**	Sweethah
Tunisia	**Túnez**	Toonayth
Turkey	**Turquía**	Toorkeeah
United States	**Estados Unidos**	Aystahdhoass ooneedhoass
Wales	**País de Gales**	Paheess day gahlayss

Ordinal numbers - Números ordinales

first	**primero**	preemayroa
second	**segundo**	saygoondoa
third	**tercero**	tehrthayroa
fourth	**cuarto**	kwahrtoa
fifth	**quinto**	keentoa
sixth	**sexto**	saykstoa
seventh	**séptimo**	saypteemoa
eighth	**octavo**	oaktahbhoa
ninth	**noveno**	noabhaynoa
tenth	**décimo**	daytheemoa
once	**una vez**	oonah bayth

twice	**dos veces**	doss baythayss
three times	**tres veces**	trayss baythayss
a half	**una mitad**	oonah meetahdh
half a ...	**medio**	maydhyoa
half of ...	**la mitad de**	lah meetahdh day
half	**medio**	maydhyoa
a quarter	**un cuarto**	oon kwahrtoa
one third	**un tercio**	oon tayrthyoa
a dozen	**una docena**	oonah dothaynah
3%	**3 por ciento**	trayss por thyayntoa

Cardinal numbers - **Números cardinales**

0	**cero**	thayroa
1	**uno**	oonoa
2	**dos**	doss
3	**tres**	trayss
4	**cuatro**	kwahtroa
5	**cinco**	theenkoa
6	**seis**	sayss
7	**siete**	seeaytay
8	**ocho**	oachoa
9	**nueve**	nwaybhay
10	**diez**	deeayth
11	**once**	onthay
12	**doce**	doathay
13	**trece**	traythay
14	**catorce**	kahtorthay
15	**quince**	keenthay
16	**dieciseis**	dyaytheessayss
17	**diecisiete**	dyaytheessyaytay
18	**dieciocho**	dyaytheeoachoa
19	**diecinueve**	dyaytheenwaybhay
20	**veinte**	bayeentay
21	**veintiuno**	baynteeoonoa
22	**veintidos**	baynteedoss

23	**veintitres**	baynteetrayss
24	**veinticuatro**	baynteekwahtroa
30	**treinta**	trayntah
40	**cuarenta**	kwahrahntah
50	**cincuenta**	theenkwayntah
60	**sesenta**	sayssayntah
70	**setenta**	saytayntah
80	**ochenta**	oachayntah
90	**noventa**	noabhayntah
100	**cien**	thyayn
200	**doscientos**	dosthyayntoass
300	**trescientos**	trayssthyayntoass
400	**cuatrocientos**	kwahtroathyayntoass
500	**quinientos**	keenyayntoass
600	**seiscientos**	sayssthyayntoass
700	**setecientos**	saytaythyayntoass
800	**ochocientos**	oachoathyayntoass
900	**novecientos**	noabhaythyayntoass
1.000	**mil**	meel

10.000	**diez mil**	dyayth meel
100.000	**cien mil**	thyayn meel
1.000.000	**un millón**	oon meelyon
1.000.000.000	**mil millones**	meel meelyoanayss

Calendar - **Calendario**

January	**Enero**	Aynayroa
February	**Febrero**	Fehbrehroa
March	**Marzo**	Mahrthoa
April	**Abril**	Ahbreel
May	**Mayo**	Mahyoa
June	**Junio**	Khoonyoa

July	**Julio**	Khoolyoa
August	**Agosto**	Ahgoastoa
September	**Septiembre**	Sehptyaymbray
October	**Octubre**	Oktoobray
November	**Noviembre**	Noabhyaymbray
December	**Diciembre**	Deethyaymbray

after June	**después de junio**	dayspwayss day khoonyoa
before July	**antes de julio**	ahntays day khoolyoa
during August	**durante agosto**	doorahntay ahgoastoa
in September	**en septiembre**	ayn sehptyaymbray

last month	**el mes pasado**	ayl mayss pahssahdhoa
next month	**el mes próximo**	ayl mayss prokseemoa
the month before	**el mes anterior**	ayl mayss ahntehryor
the month after	**el mes siguiente**	ayl mayss seegyayntay

at the beginning of January	**a principios de enero**	ah preentheepyoass day aynayroa
in the middle of february	**a mediados de febrero**	ah maydhyahdhoass day fehbrehroa
at the end of March	**a finales de marzo**	ah feenahlayss day mahrthoa

Seasons - **Estaciones**

spring	**la primavera**	lah preemahbhayrah
summer	**el verano**	ayl bayrahnoa
autumn	**el otoño**	ayl otoañoa
winter	**el invierno**	ayl eenbyayrnoa
in spring	**en primavera**	ayn preemahbhayrah
high season	**estación alta**	aystahthyon ahltah
low season	**estación baja**	aystahthyon bahkha

Dates - **Fechas**

What´s the date today?	**¿En qué fecha estamos?**	ayn kay faychah aystahmoass?
When's your birthday?	**¿Cuándo es su cumpleaños?**	kwahndoa ayss soo koomplayahnyoass?
August 1st	**el uno de agosto**	ayl oonoa day ahgoastoa
May 10th	**el diez de mayo**	ayl dyayth day mahyoa

Days of the week - **Días de la semana**

What day is it today?	**¿Qué día es hoy?**	Kay deeah ayss oy?
Sunday	**domingo**	doameengoa
Monday	**lunes**	loonayss
Tuesday	**martes**	mahrtayss
Wednesday	**miércoles**	myayrkoalayss
Thursday	**jueves**	khwaybhayss
Friday	**viernes**	Byayrnayss
Saturday	**sábado**	Sahbhadhoa
in the morning	**por la mañana**	por lah manyahnah
during the day	**durante el día**	doorahntay ayl deeah
in the afternoon	**por la tarde**	por lah tahrday
in the evening	**por la tarde**	por lah tahrday
at night	**por la noche**	por lah noachay

| at dawn | **al amanecer** | ahl ahmahnaythayr |
| at dusk | **al anochecer** | ahl ahnoachaythayr |

Miscellaneous

yesterday	**ayer**	ahyehr
today	**hoy**	oy
tomorrow	**mañana**	manyahnah
the day before	**el día anterior**	ayl deeah ahntehryor
the next day	**el día siguiente**	ayl deeah seegyayntay
two days ago	**hace dos días**	ahthay doss deeahss
in three days' time	**en tres días**	ayn trayss deeahss
last week	**la semana pasada**	lah saymahnah pahssahdhah
next week	**la semana próxima**	lah saymahnah prokseemah
in two weeks	**por una quincena**	por oonah keenthehnah
birthday	**el cumpleaños**	ayl koomplayahnyoass
the day	**el día**	ayl deeah
the day off	**el día libre**	ayl deeah leebray
holiday	**el día festivo**	ayl deeah faysteebhoa
holidays	**las vacaciones**	lahss bahkahthyonayss
school holidays	**las vacaciones del colegio**	lahss bahkahthyonayss dayl koalekhyoa
week	**la semana**	lah saymahnah
weekday	**el día de la semana**	ayl deeah day lah saymahnah
weekend	**el fin de semana**	ayl feen day sahmahnah
working day	**el día laborable**	ayl deeah lahbhoarahblay

Warnings/Notices - Avisos

Down	**Abajo**	ahbahkhoa
Open	**Abierto**	ahbyayrtoa
Up	**Arriba**	ahrreebah
Lift/elevator	**Ascensor**	ahsthaynsoar
Out of order	**Averiado**	ahbayrahdoa
Gentlemen	**Caballeros**	kahbahlyayroass
Cash desk	**Caja**	kahkhah
Hot	**Caliente**	kahlyayntay
Private road	**Carretera particular**	kahrraytayrah pahrteekoolahr
Closed	**Cerrado**	thayrrahdhoa
Close the door	**Cierre la puerta**	thyayrray lah pwayrtah
No vacancy	**Completo**	komplaytoa
Caution	**Cuidado**	kweedhahdhoa
Beware of the dog	**Cuidado con el perro**	kweedhahdhoa kon ayl payrroa
Push	**Empujar**	aympookhahr
Entrance	**Entrada**	ayntrahdhah
Admission free	**Entrada libre**	ayntrahdhah leebray
Enter without knocking	**Entre sin llamar**	ayntray seen lyahmahr
Cold	**Frío**	freeoa

Vacant	**Libre**	leebray
Do not disturb	**No molestar**	noa moalaystahr
Do not block entrance	**No obstruya la entrada**	noa oabstrooyah lah ayntrahdah
Do not touch	**No tocar**	noa toakahr
Occupied	**Ocupado**	oakoopahdhoa
Danger	**Peligro**	payleegroa
Danger of death	**Peligro de muerte**	payleegroa day mwayrtay
Wet paint	**Pintura fresca**	peentoorah frayskah
Private	**Privado**	preebahdhoa
No littering	**Prohibido arrojar basuras**	proaeebheedhoa ahrroakhahr bahssoorahs
No entry	**Prohibido entrar**	proaeebheedhoa ayntrahr
No smoking	**Prohibido fumar**	proaeebheedhoa foomahr
No trespassing	**Prohibida la entrada a personas no autorizadas**	proaeebheedhah lah ayntrahdhah ah payrsoanahs noa owtoareethahdhahss
Sale	**Rebajas**	raybahkhahss
Reserved	**Reservado**	raysayrbahdhoa
Waiting room	**Sala de espera**	sahlah day ayspayrah
Exit	**Salida**	sahleedhah
Emergency exit	**Salida de emergencia**	sahleedhah dah aymayrkhayntheeah
To let (for rent)	**Se alquila**	say ahlkeelah
For sale	**Se vende**	say byanday
Bicycle path	**Sendero para bicicletas**	sayndayroa pahrah beetheeklaytahss
Ladies	**Señoras**	sayñoarahss
Toilets	**Servicios**	sehrbeethyoass
Pull	**Tirar**	teerahr
Please ring	**Toque el timbre, por favor**	toakay ayl teembray, por fahbhor

Usual phrases - Frases usuales
Greetings - Saludos

Good morning	**Buenos días**	Bwaynoass deeahss
Good evening	**Buenas tardes**	Bwaynahss tahrdayss
Good night	**Buenas noches**	Bwaynahs notchayss
Hello! Hi!	**¿Qué hay?, ¿Qué tal?**	Kay I? Kay tahl?
How are you?	**¿Cómo está usted?**	Komoa aystah oostayd?
Very well, thank you	**Muy bien, gracias**	Mwee byayn, grahthyahss
See you tomorrow	**Hasta mañana**	Ahstah manyahnah
Good bye	**Adiós**	Ahdyoass
See you soon	**Hasta pronto**	Ahstah prontoa
How do you do?	**Tanto gusto**	Tantoa goostoa

Questions - Preguntas

Do you speak Spanish?	¿Habla usted español?	Ahblah oostayd espanyohl?
Do you understand?	¿Comprende usted?	Komprenday oostayd?
What did you say?	¿Cómo ha dicho?	Komoa ah deechoa?
What are you saying?	¿Qué dice usted?	Kay deethay oostayd?
Pardon?	¿Cómo dice?	Komoa deethay?
Who is it?	¿Quién es?	Kyayn ayss?
What is that?	¿Qué es eso?	Kay ayss ayssoa?
Where are you going?	¿Dónde va usted?	Donday vah oostayd?
What do you want?	¿Qué quiere usted?	Kay kyayray oostayd?
Are you sure?	¿Está usted seguro?	Aystah oostayd saygooroa?
Really?	¿De veras?	Day verahss?
How much?	¿Cuánto?	Kwahntoa?
How many?	¿Cuántos?	Kwahntoass?
Here or there?	¿Aquí o allá?	Ahkee oh alyah?
Why?	¿Por qué?	Porr kay?

Introductions - Presentaciones

Let me introduce you to Mr. ...	Le presento al Sr...	Lay praysayntoa al saynyorr ...
Glad to see you	Mucho gusto	Moochoa goostoa
My name is	Me llamo	May lyahmoa

Politeness - Cortesía

Cheers!	A su salud	Ah soo sahlood
With pleasure	Con mucho gusto	Kon moochoa goostoa
Excuse me	Dispense	Despaynsay
You are very kind	Es usted muy amable	Ayss oostaid moy ahmahblay

Thank you	Gracias	Grahthyahss
Thank you very much	Muchas gracias	Moochahs grahthyahss
Sorry	Perdón	Perrdohn
Please	Por favor	Porr fahvorr
Sit down, please	Siéntese, por favor	Syentaysay, porr fahvorr

Adjectives and pronouns - Adjetivos y pronombres

Possessive adjectives - Adjetivos posesivos

My	Mi	Mee
Your	Tu	Too

His/Her/Its	Su	Soo
Our	Nuestro	Nooaystroa

Your	Vuestro	Vooaystroa
Their	Su	Soo

Demonstrative pronouns - Pronombres demostrativos

This	Éste	Aystay
That	Ése	Ayssay
That	Aquél	Ahkayl
These	Éstos	Aystoass
Those	Ésos	Aysoass
Those	Aquéllos	Ahkaylyoass

Possessive pronouns - Pronombres posesivos

Mine	Mío	Meeoa
Yours	Tuyo	Tooyoa
His/Hers/Its	Suyo	Sooyoa
Ours	Nuestro	Nooaystroa
Yours	Vuestro	Vooaystroa
Theirs	Suyo	Sooyoa

Verb To Be - Verbo Ser

Present	Presente	Present Perfect	Pretérito Perfecto
I am	Yo soy	I have been	Yo he sido
You are	Tú eres	You have been	Tú has sido
He / She / It is	El / Ella / Usted es	He/She/It has been	El / Ella / Usted ha sido
We are	Nosotros somos	We have been	Nosotros hemos sido
You are	Vosotros sois	You have been	Vosotros habéis sido
They are	Ellos / Ellas / Ustedes son	They have been	Ellos/Ellas/Ustedes han sido

Past simple	Imperfecto	Past perfect	Pluscuamperfecto
I was	Yo era	I had been	Yo había sido
You were	Tú eras	You had been	Tú habías sido
He/She/It was	El/Ella/Usted era	He/She/It had been	El/Ella/Usted había sido
We were	Nosotros éramos	We had been	Nosotros habíamos sido
You were	Vosotros erais	You had been	Vosotros habíais sido
They were	Ellos/Ellas/Ustedes eran	They had been	Ellos/Ellas/Ustedes habían sido

Past simple	Indefinido	Past perfect	Anterior
I was	Yo fui	I had been	Yo hube sido
You were	Tú fuiste	You had been	Tú hubiste sido
He/She/It was	El/Ella/Usted fue	He / She/It had been	El/Ella/Usted hubo sido
We were	Nosotros fuimos	We had been	Nosotros hubimos sido
You were	Vosotros fuisteis	You had been	Vosotros hubisteis sido
They were	Ellos/Ellas/Ustedes fueron	They had been	Ellos/Ellas/Ustedes hubieron sido

Future simple	Futuro	Future perfect	Futuro perfecto
I will be	Yo seré	I will have been	Yo habré sido
You will be	Tú serás	You will have been	Tú habrás sido
He/She/It will be	El / Ella / Usted será	He/She/It will have been	El / Ella / Usted habrá sido
We will be	Nosotros seremos	We will have been	Nosotros habremos sido
You will be	Vosotros seréis	You will have been	Vosotros habréis sido
They will be	Ellos/Ellas/Ustedes serán	They will have been	Ellos/Ellas/Ustedes

Verb To Be - Verbo Estar

Present	Presente	Present Perfect	Pretérito Perfecto
I am	Yo estoy	I have been	Yo he estado
You are	Tú estás	You have been	Tú has estado
He / She / It is	El/Ella/Usted está	He/She/ It has been	El / Ella / Usted ha estado
We are	Nosotros estamos	We have been	Nosotros hemos estado
You are	Vosotros estáis	You have been	Vosotros habéis estado
They are	Ellos/Ellas/Ustedes están	They have been	Ellos/Ellas/Ustedes han estado

Miscellaneous

Past simple	Imperfecto
I was	Yo estaba
You were	Tú estabas
He/She/It was	El/Ella/Usted estaba
We were	Nosotros stábamos
You were	Vosotros estabais
They were	Ellos/Ellas/Ustedes estaban

Past perfect	Pluscuamperfecto
I had been	Yo había estado
You had been	Tú habías estado
He/She/It had been	El/Ella/Usted había estado
We had been	Nosotros habíamos estado
You had been	Vosotros habíais estado
They had been	Ellos/Ellas/Ustedes habían estado

Past simple	Indefinido
I was	Yo estuve
You were	Tú estuviste
He/She/It was	El/Ella/Usted estuvo
We were	Nosotros estuvimos
You were	Vosotros estuvisteis
They were	Ellos/Ellas/Ustedes estuvieron

Past perfect	Anterior
I had been	Yo hube estado
You had been	Tú hubiste estado
He/She/It had been	El/Ella/Usted hubo estado
We had been	Nosotros hubimos estado
You had been	Vosotros hubisteis estado
They had been	Ellos/Ellas/Ustedes hubieron estado

Future simple	Futuro
I will be	Yo estaré
You will be	Tú estarás
He/She/It will be	El / Ella / Usted estará
We will be	Nosotros estaremos
You will be	Vosotros estaréis
They will be	Ellos/Ellas/Ustedes estarán

Future perfect	Futuro perfecto
I will have been	Yo habré estado
You will have been	Tú habrás estado
He / She / It will have been	El/Ella/Usted habrá estado
We will have been	Nosotros habremos estado
You will have been	Vosotros habréis estado
They will have been	Ellos/Ellas/Ustedes habrán estado

Verb To Have - Verbo Tener

Present	Presente
I have	Yo tengo
You have	Tú tienes
He /She / It has	El/Ella/Usted tiene
We have	Nosotros tenemos
You have	Vosotros tenéis
They have	Ellos/Ellas/Ustedes tienen

Present perfect	Pret. Perfecto
I have had	Yo he tenido
You have had	Tú has tenido
He/She/It has had	El / Ella / Usted ha tenido
We have had	Nosotros hemos tenido
You have had	Vosotros habéis tenido
They have had	Ellos/Ellas/Ustedes han tenido

Past simple	Imperfecto
I had	Yo tenía
You had	Tú tenías
He/She/It had	El / Ella /Usted tenía
We had	Nosotros teníamos
You had	Vosotros teníais
They had	Ellos/Ellas/Ustedes tenían

Past perfect	Pluscuamperfecto
I had had	Yo había tenido
You had had	Tú habías tenido
He/ She/It had had	El / Ella / Usted había tenido
We had had	Nosotros habíamos tenido
You had had	Vosotros habíais tenido
They had had	Ellos/Ellas/Ustedes habían tenido

Miscellaneous

Past simple	Indefinido
had	Yo tuve
you had	Tú tuviste
He/She/It had	El/Ella/Usted tuvo
We had	Nosotros tuvimos
You had	Vosotros tuvisteis
They had	Ellos/Ellas/Ustedes tuvieron

Past perfect	Anterior
I had had	Yo hube tenido
You had had	Tú hubiste tenido
He/She/It had had	El/Ella/Usted hubo tenido
We had had	Nosotros hubimos tenido
You had had	Vosotros hubisteis tenido
They had had	Ellos/Ellas/Ustedes hubieron tenido

Future simple	Futuro
will have	Yo tendré
you will have	Tú tendrás
He / She / It will have	El / Ella / Usted tendrá
We will have	Nosotros tendremos
you will have	Vosotros tendréis
They will have	Ellos/Ellas/Ustedes tendrán

Future perfect	Futuro perfecto
I will have had	Yo habré tenido
You will have had	Tú habrás tenido
He / She / It will have had	El / Ella / Usted habrá tenido
We will have had	Nosotros habremos tenido
You will have had	Vosotros habréis tenido
They will have had	Ellos/Ellas/Ustedes habrán tenido

Times Differences of G.M.T. in relation with other countries

Country	GMT	Country	GMT	Country	GMT	Country	GMT
Aden	-1	Congo (Leopolville)	+1	Irak	+3 ½	Saudi Arabia	+3
Afghanistan	+4 ½	Chile	-4	Israel	+2	Singapur	+5 ½
Germany	+1	Costa Rica	-6	Italy	+1	South Africa	+2
Algeria	+ 1	Cuba	-5	Jamaica	-5	Sweden	+1
Argentina	-3	Czechoslovakia	+1	Japan	+9	Switzerland	+1
Australia (Victoria)	+10	Denmark	+1	Kenya	+3	Syria	+2
Austria	+1	Ecuador	-5	Madagascar	+3	Tanganika	+3
Belgium	+1	Egypt	+2	Malaya	+7 ½	Thailand	+7
Bermudas	-4	Spain	+1	Mexico	-6	Trinidad	-4
Bolivia	-4	Philippines	+8	Mozambique	+2	Turkey	+2
Borneo	+8	Finland	+2	New Zealand	+12	Uganda	+3
Brazil (East)	-3	France	+1	Nigeria	+11	Russia	+3
Brazil (West)	-4	Great Britain	0	Norway	+1	USA (East)	-5
Bulgaria	+2	Greece	+2	Pakistan	+5	USA (Centre)	-6
Canada (Atlantic)	-4	Netherlands	+1	Panama	-5	USA (Pacific)	-7
Canada (Pacific)	-8	Hong-Kong	+8	Paraguay	-4	USA (West Coast)	-8
Canarias	0	Hungary	+1	Peru	-5	USA (Alaska)	-11
Ceylon	+5 ½	India	+5 ½	Poland	+1	USA (Hawai)	-10
Colombia	-5	Indonesia (Java)	+7 ½	Portugal	+1	Uruguay	-3
		Iran	+3 ½	Rodesia	+2	Venezuela	-4 ½
				Rumania	+2		

Miscellaneous

Money - Monedas

Argentina	**peso**	Rep. Dominicana	**peso**	Paraguay	**guaraní**	
Bolivia	**boliviano**	Ecuador	**sucre**	Perú	**sol**	
Brasil	**cruzeiro**	España	**euro**	Puerto Rico	**dólar de los**	
Colombia	**peso**	Guatemala	**quetzal**		**Estados Unidos**	
Costa Rica	**colón**	Honduras	**lempira**			
Cuba	**peso**	Méjico	**peso**	El Salvador	**colón**	
Chile	**peso**	Nicaragua	**córdoba**	Uruguay	**peso**	
		Panamá	**balboa**	Venezuela	**bolívar**	

Equivalence - Equivalencia

Measures of surface

144 square inches	= 1 square foot
9 square feet	= 1 square yard
30 1/2 square yards	= 1 square vara
40 square varas	= 1 rood
4 roods	= 1 acre
4,840 square yards	= 1 acre
640 acres	= 1 square mile

Measures of weight

437,7 grains	= 1 onza
16 ounces	= 1 libra
14 pounds	= 1 stone
28 pounds	= 1 quarter
4 quarters	= 1 hundredweight
20 hundredweight	= 1 ton

Measures of volume

1,728 cubic inches	= 1 cubic foot
27 cubic feet	= 1 cubic yard
5,8 cubic feet	= 1 bulk barrel

Measures of capacity

1 fluid dracma	= 1 fluid ounce
5 fluid ounces	= 1 gill
2 gills	= 1 pint
2 pints	= 1 quart.
4 quart	= 1 imperial gallon
2 gallons	= 1 peck
4 pecks	= 1 bushel
8 bushels	= 1 quarter
36 gallons	= 1 bulk barrel

Volume

1 cubic foot	= 28,31 dm^3
1 dm	= 61,023 cubic inches

Other measures

1 ton reg.	= 100 cubic feet
1 knot	= 1 nautical mile per hour
1 nautical mile	= 6,080 feet
6 feet	= 1 fathom
1 league	= 3 nautical miles

Measures of length

12 inches	= 1 foot
3 feet	= 1 yard
5 1/2 yards	= 1 vara
4 varas	= 1 chain
10 chains	= 1 stadium
8 stadia	= 1 mile

Miscellaneous

Distances, measures and weights - Distancia medidas y pesos

Kilometres to miles / 1 kilometre (km.) = 0.62 miles

km.	10	20	30	40	50	60	70	80	90	100	110	120	130
miles	6	12	19	25	31	37	44	50	56	62	68	75	81

Miles to kilometres / 1 mile = 1.609 kilometres (km.)

miles	10	20	30	40	50	60	70	80	90	100
km.	16	32	48	64	80	97	113	129	145	161

Measures of liquids / 1 litre (l.) = 0.88 imp. quarts = 1.06 U.S. quarts

1 imp.quart = 1.14 l. / 1 U.S.quart = 0.95 l. / 1 imp.gallon = 4.55 l. / 1 U.S.gallon = 3.8 l.

l.	5	10	15	20	25	30	35	40	45	50
imp. gal.	1.1	2.2	3.3	4.4	5.5	6.6	7.7	8.8	9.9	11.0
U.S. gal.	1.3	2.6	3.9	5.2	6.5	7.8	9.1	10.4	11.7	13.0

Weights and measures / 1 kilogram or kilo (kg.) = 1000 grammes (g.)

100g. = 3.5 oz. / ½kg. = 1.1lb. / 1oz. = 28.35g. / 1kg. = 2.2lb. / 1lb. = 453.60g.

Length

1 inch (pulgada)	= 25,4 mm
1 foot (pie)	= 0,3048 m
1 yard (yarda)	= 0,9144 m
1 mile (milla)	= 1,609 km
1 cm = 0,3937 inches	= 0,03280 feet
1 m = 3,2808 feet	=1,0936 yards
1 km = 0,62137 miles	

Capacity

1 quart (USA)	= 0,9463 litros
1 quart (G.B.)	= 1,1364 litros
1 pint (USA)	= 0,4731 litros
1 pint (G.B.)	= 0,5682 litros
1 gallon (USA)	= 3,7853 litros
1 gallon (G.B.)	= 4,546 litros
1 bushel (USA)	=35,2382 litros
1 bushel (G.B.)	=36,3676 litros
1 litre	= 0,212 gallons G.B.
	= 0,264 gallons USA
	= 1,756 pints G.B.

Surface

1 square foot	= 0,093 m^2
1 square yard	= 0,8361 m^2
1 acre	= 0,4047 Ha
1 m^2	= 10,764 square feet
1 área	= 1.076,4 square feet
	= 0,02471 acres

Weight

1 pound	= 0,4536 kg
1 pound	= 0,3732 kg
1 ounce	= 28,35 g
1 onza	= 31,10 g
1 kg	= 35,274 ounces
1 kg	= 2,205 pounds

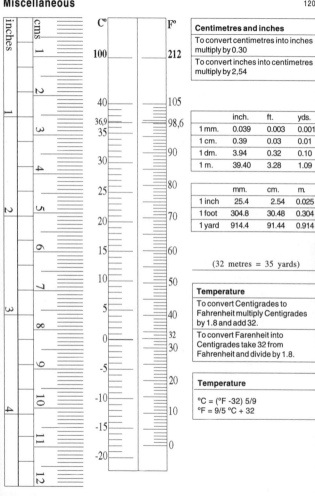

Centimetres and inches

To convert centimetres into inches multiply by 0.30
To convert inches into centimetres multiply by 2,54

	inch.	ft.	yds.
1 mm.	0.039	0.003	0.001
1 cm.	0.39	0.03	0.01
1 dm.	3.94	0.32	0.10
1 m.	39.40	3.28	1.09

	mm.	cm.	m.
1 inch	25.4	2.54	0.025
1 foot	304.8	30.48	0.304
1 yard	914.4	91.44	0.914

(32 metres = 35 yards)

Temperature

To convert Centigrades to Fahrenheit multiply Centigrades by 1.8 and add 32.
To convert Farenheit into Centigrades take 32 from Fahrenheit and divide by 1.8.

Temperature

°C = (°F -32) 5/9
°F = 9/5 °C + 32

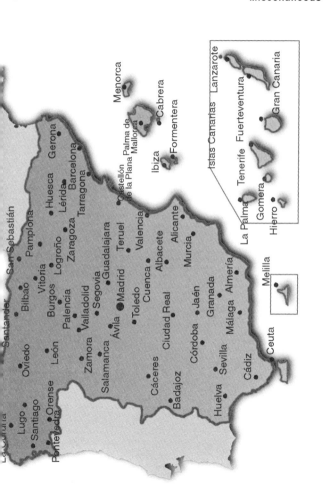